D1744669

Sir Walter Stanford

His Forebears and Family

Sir Walter Stanford

His Forebears and Family

CELIA EDEY

Published by Celia Edey
www.sirwalterstanford.co.uk
celia@sirwalterstanford.co.uk

First edition 2017

Sir Walter Stanford: His Forebears and Family
ISBN 978-0-620-76586-2

Copyright © 2017 Celia Edey

All rights reserved. No part of this publication may be reproduced,
stored in a retrieval system, or transmitted, in any form or by any means, without
the prior written permission of the publisher.

Book design: Vanessa Wilson
Cover concept: Celia Edey
Production assistant: Lindsay Green
Typesetting and production: Quickfox Publishing
Printed by Digital Action SA, Cape Town, South Africa

This book is dedicated to my grandmother,
Dorothy Maud Ruffel (née Stanford);
my mother,
Frances Marjory Lois Green (née Ruffel);
and my daughter,
Kate Audrey Mozzicarelli (née Edey).

All of them have had a deep interest in family history.
All of them have given me immense love and joy.
All of them have inspired me.

Acknowledgements

In preparing this book, I have consulted many of my cousins and incorporated as many of their personal comments as possible. Notable amongst them have been Bruce, Allison, John, and Helen Pat (grandchildren of Ganku's), Jan, Bina, Bron, Michele, Veronique, Micky, Jonathon, Oliver and Diana (some of his great-grandchildren). I am particularly grateful for Micky's permission to include the wonderful stories and sketches done by her grandfather, Walter Elliot Stanford.

I have spent many hours in the University of Cape Town Archive Library poring over the Walter Stanford collection for which I am grateful.

My brother, Malcolm, has given me constant encouragement, advice and suggestions, and my husband, Russell, has given me much useful constructive criticism, and has been endlessly tolerant of my preoccupation in my task!

It was my mother, Lois, and grandmother, Dorothy, who displayed the love and pride in Ganku which led me to try and discover more about his personality and about his family. The desire to capture this for following generations, and in particular, my own children Philip, Kate and Anthony and their families, drove me ever onwards.

Contents

Introduction   page 9

Chapter I   page 11   A Brief Summary of the 1820 Settler Scheme

Chapter II   page 16   **The 1820 Settler Generation**
                                              John and Maria Stanford
                                              Henry and Elizabeth Warner
                                              Joseph and Margaret Walker
                                              Edward and Anne Driver

Chapter III   page 28   **The First Generation Born in South Africa**
                                              William and Joanna Rosina Stanford – Walter's parents
                                              Joseph Cox Warner – Walter's uncle
                                              Joseph and Dorothy Walker – Sarah Alice Stanford's parents

Chapter IV   page 33   **The Second Generation Born in South Africa**
                                              Robert and Arthur Stanford – Walter's brothers

Chapter V   page 40   **Walter Ernest Mortimer Stanford**
                   page 64   His obituary

Chapter VI   page 66   **Sarah Alice Stanford (née Walker) – His Wife**

Chapter VII   page 72   **The Third Generation Born in South Africa**
                                              Sir Walter and Lady Stanford's children:
                   page 72   Walter Elliot
                   page 77   Dorothy Maud
                   page 83   Robert Cecil
                   page 84   Alice Minnie
                   page 88   Arthur Warner
                   page 91   Helen Rose
                   page 95   Eileen Mary

Chapter VIII   page 98   **A Personal Afterword**

Appendix I   page 100   **The Wider Family**
First Generation
Walter's uncles and aunts
Sarah Alice's uncles and aunts

page 101   *Second Generation*
Walter's half-siblings
Walter's cousins
Sarah Alice's siblings

Appendix II   page 106   **Some More About Ganku**

Appendix III   page 112   **Stories Written by Walter Elliot Stanford**

Appendix IV   page 129   **Descendant Trees of Walter Ernest Mortimer Stanford's Children**

page 136   Bibliography

page 137   Illustrations and photographs

Introduction

This is the story of one family in South Africa in the 19th and 20th centuries. The central character is my great-grandfather, Sir Walter Ernest Mortimer Stanford, who was much-loved and who is remembered with pride by his descendants.

Walter left school at the age of 12, speaking Xhosa as fluently as he spoke English. He immediately embarked on a career which eventually included being magistrate to the Thembu and a member of the Native Laws and Customs Commission when he was only 30 years old; Chief Magistrate of the Transkeian Territories; a member of the South African Native Affairs Commission from 1903–1905; a senator and the Commissioner of Returning Soldiers after the World War I. He was knighted for this last role. However, arguably his greatest contribution to his country was as a member of the National Convention of 1908–1909, which led to the Union of South Africa. During the debate on the future constitution, he advocated for universal franchise, irrespective of race or colour.

He and his wife, Sarah Alice (née Walker), were both descended from 1820 settlers – also a matter of family pride. My mother told us many stories from her own childhood, which seemed, from the comfort of our familiar English house and garden, to have been lived in extraordinary wildness and freedom, even with a touch of pioneering about them. How much greater courage and determination must have been demanded of her forebears. They arrived in undeveloped parts of the Cape Colony with virtually nothing, only to find difficult terrain, justifiably resentful tribesman just out of sight and very little means to build even the most basic house.

Where did that pioneering spirit come from, and what were the stories of those ancestors who first made that arduous and dangerous journey? How did the generations, from humble beginnings, carve out distinguished careers and great achievements? What made them stand out from the crowd?

The van Riebeeck Society, founded in 1918 with the purpose of making primary sources available in a readable and enjoyable form to anyone interested in Southern African history, published two volumes of *Stanford's Reminiscences*, with help from my grandmother, Dorothy Maud Ruffel. These provide great detail of Sir Walter Ernest Mortimer Stanford's career; largely drawn from Walter's own diaries. However, they include very little family or personal detail. It is this that I seek to do, drawing together all my maternal ancestors and giving colour to my family tree.

Many of the quotes in this book reflect the phraseology and words of a 150 years ago. I have not attempted to change them, but they are not the words I would now use. Some family anecdotes, passed from generation to generation by word-of-mouth and often told with humour, display attitudes that now seem shocking. I do not defend these, but I remember the historical context and the mores pertaining to the time.

While our ancestors were of their time, many of them showed greater compassion, understanding and respect for the indigenous people of South Africa than most of their contemporaries. I believe their liberalism took courage, and it is this that allows my continued pride in them.

Celia Edey, April 2017

CHAPTER I

A Brief Summary of the 1820 Settler Scheme

In 1795 the French invaded Holland and laid claim to her overseas possessions. The British, however, were determined to keep the Cape out of French hands and sent a squadron of ships to Cape Town. They defeated the Dutch and took possession of the Cape Colony. Five years later, the Dutch East India Company, then old and corrupt, went bankrupt. In 1802, after a treaty was signed between Britain and France, the British handed the Cape back to the government of Holland, which had become the Batavian Republic.

However, this arrangement was short-lived. By 1806 Napoleon was running rampant and Britain and France were once again at war. Britain sent another squadron of ships to seize the Cape and keep it from the French. The Cape Colony remained in British hands until it was incorporated into the Union of South Africa in 1910. South Africa subsequently became a republic in 1961.

Between 1779 and 1818, as a result of boundary disputes, there were five wars between the Xhosa people and the white farmers in the Eastern Cape. The Dutch farmers knew the land in this area was better suited to stock farming than to cultivation, but Xhosa cattle raiding discouraged them from embarking on this type of farming.

Governor of the Cape Lord Charles Somerset proposed an agricultural settlement there as a 'buffer' between the Xhosas and the Cape Colony, which would reduce the need for the military to maintain the frontier. After the Napoleonic Wars, there was a growing unemployment problem in Britain, caused in part by 300 000 British soldiers and sailors looking for employment, and in part by the widespread use of children as labourers, which lead to a shortage of work for adults. In addition, laws had been passed that allowed wealthy landowners the right to fence off their land and charge people to use it for their animals and crops.

Lord Charles Somerset

Villagers were forced to pay rent to the landowners, or to work for them. Somerset's scheme was agreed upon in July 1819, and planning was immediately set in motion.

To encourage settlers to come forward, the government promised people their own farms in Africa, and encouraged a belief that starting a new life in a new land held a romantic appeal for the many who were struggling to make a living in Britain. The prospective settlers were not told that they would be moving into disputed territory and an area prone to drought. They were informed that the countryside resembled English parkland which, in years of good rainfall, was true.

The scheme was limited to men who could afford to engage and maintain a party of at least 10 able-bodied labourers over the age of 18 (with or without families) from whom deposits were demanded. In return, the party leader would receive free passage and 'victuals' and be granted 100 acres of land in the Eastern Cape plus 100 acres per man in their party. The government was bombarded with applications. An estimated 90 000 were received. In the end, about 4 000 settlers were accepted. They made up 61 'parties', of which four consisted of the poor, for which parishes had raised the money and assisted with their deposits.

This scale model was built by Dr J.A. Pringle of the Port Elizabeth Museum. It is based on the only known plans of a settler ship to have survived.

They were to be transported in ships from the navy, and some troop ships had to be refurbished to make them more comfortable and suitable for the transportation of civilians. The *Weymouth* was one such ship. It was docked next to a 'hulk' while work was carried out on it.

As settlers began to arrive in Deptford, they were accommodated on the hulk until the *Weymouth* was ready for boarding. The ships were to sail in pairs, but even though they set off together, weather and sea conditions meant they did not arrive at the same times. The first ships set sail on 3 December 1819 and the first arrived at their destination, Algoa Bay (later to become Port Elizabeth), in early April 1820.

During the journey most of the ships called in to the Cape Verde Islands to restock their rations, and purchase fresh fruit, vegetables and some meat. Water was rationed to less than three and a half litres per person per day for drinking and washing purposes. In addition, men were given a tot of rum, and ladies were allowed tea instead! Strict rules dictated when everyone had to get up. Bedding had to be rolled up and partitions taken down every morning; trunks had to be stored away, and washing could only be done at certain times. However, there was plenty of free time and life settled into a 'normal' routine as groups got to know their neighbours.

The ships were greeted at Table Bay by Deputy Colonial Secretary Henry Ellis and other senior officials. One can imagine the excitement and awe among the settlers as the ships arrived in Table Bay and they caught their first glimpse of the magnificent mountains of the Cape. Algoa Bay, on the other hand, would have been a stark contrast and disappointment, with sand everywhere and only a few buildings dotting the landscape, such as Fort Frederick. Their dismay would have increased when they were transferred to boats and rowed ashore. Sometimes they were then transferred to other smaller flat-bottomed boats before being carried ashore by the Hottentots and soldiers who had been engaged to assist with this task.

At least 2 000 tents were eventually pitched on the beach at Algoa Bay, and it became a bustling tented camp for the settlers while they waited to be taken up country to their allocated settlements around Albany. For this journey, Boer (Dutch) wagon drivers were employed. Some took the direct route to Grahamstown; while others took longer. Good rains had just fallen and the countryside was quite beautiful. However, dotted along the routes could be seen abandoned and often blackened gables of deserted houses: signs of troubled times, and perhaps a frightening omen for the newcomers.

From Albany, they were taken to and dropped off at their locations with all their belongings. They set to building simple houses, either from reeds or using the British wattle-and-daub method. They also began to plant their crops with the seed they had bought on arrival in Algoa Bay. They soon discovered the ploughs they had brought with them were inadequate to till very hard, stony ground, and many sought help from the Boers. However, the first wheat crops began to appear, and everything looked lush and green. Their hopes were quickly dashed when the crops were destroyed by rust: a disease contained in the seed they had bought.

Settlers arriving in Algoa Bay, 1820

It also quickly became apparent that 100 acres for crops was not sufficient land to provide a sustainable living. With two subsequent crops failing through drought, many of the settlers moved away from the land and tried to establish themselves in occupations in the towns. For this reason, the frontier areas were never as densely populated as Lord Somerset had planned. Those who remained as farmers, made a significant contribution to agriculture by planting maize, rye and barley. They also started wool farming which, in time, became a very lucrative trade. Trading by the settlers contributed to business and the economy, and new towns, such as Grahamstown and Port Elizabeth, grew rapidly.

With the establishment of schools and churches for the settlers in the Cape, the Afrikaners (former Dutch settlers) felt dissatisfaction with the Anglicisation, and that their language was in danger of becoming extinct. At the same time, unrest on the eastern border became worse and caused unease between the Xhosas and the settlers. Despite the establishment of neutral zones, violence and fighting could not be prevented, and the settlers had to find new ways to stay alive.

Many Afrikaans farmers left the eastern border to establish independent states in the interior – a migration that was later referred to as the Great Trek. It was an historical event that greatly determined the shape and structure of the South Africa of the future. The other significant event was Mfecane – a period of widespread chaos and warfare among indigenous ethnic communities in southern Africa during the period between 1815 and 1840.

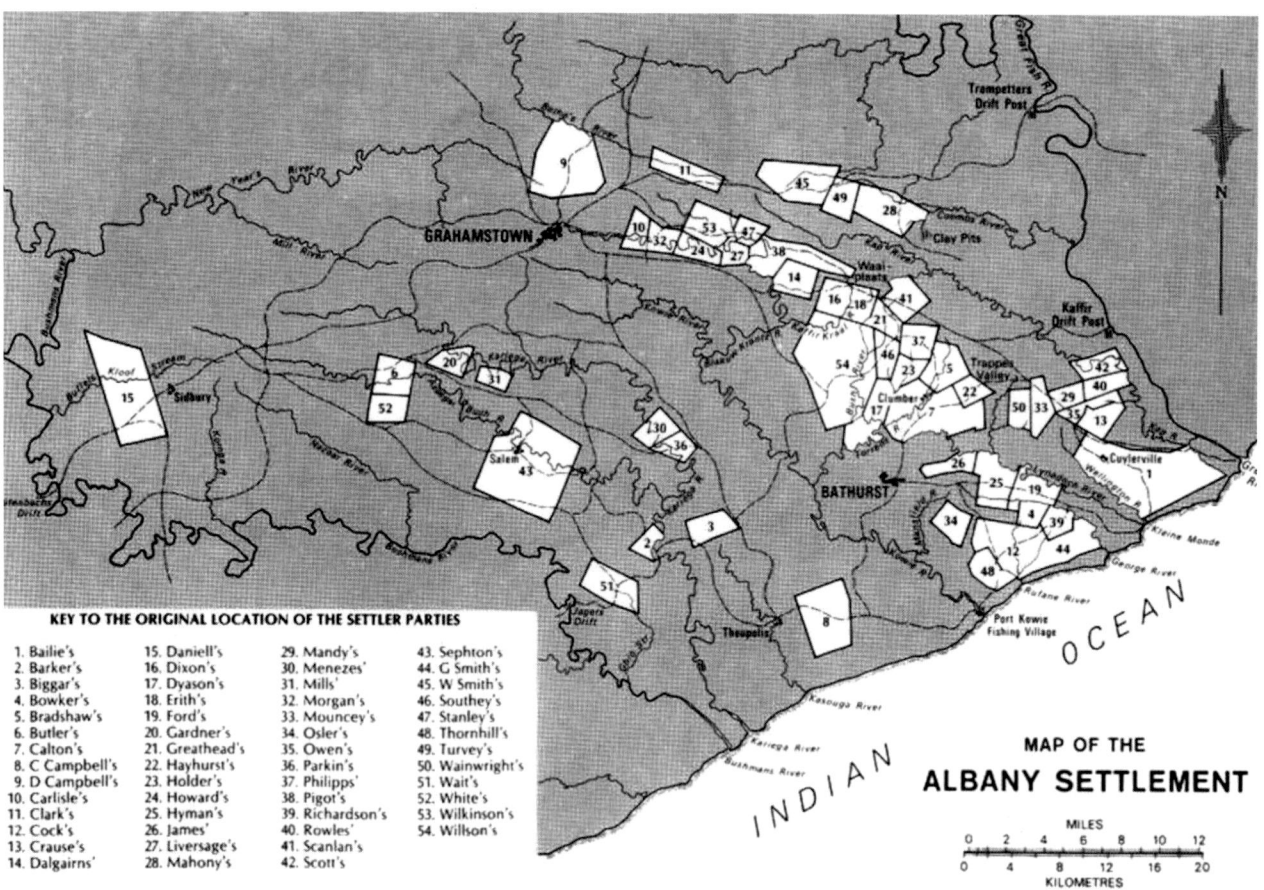

KEY TO THE ORIGINAL LOCATION OF THE SETTLER PARTIES

1. Bailie's	15. Daniell's	29. Mandy's	43. Sephton's
2. Barker's	16. Dixon's	30. Menezes'	44. G Smith's
3. Biggar's	17. Dyason's	31. Mills'	45. W Smith's
4. Bowker's	18. Erith's	32. Morgan's	46. Southey's
5. Bradshaw's	19. Ford's	33. Mouncey's	47. Stanley's
6. Butler's	20. Gardner's	34. Osler's	48. Thornhill's
7. Calton's	21. Greathead's	35. Owen's	49. Turvey's
8. C Campbell's	22. Hayhurst's	36. Parkin's	50. Wainwright's
9. D Campbell's	23. Holder's	37. Philipps'	51. Wait's
10. Carlisle's	24. Howard's	38. Pigot's	52. White's
11. Clark's	25. Hyman's	39. Richardson's	53. Wilkinson's
12. Cock's	26. James'	40. Rowles'	54. Willson's
13. Crause's	27. Liversage's	41. Scanlan's	
14. Dalgairns'	28. Mahony's	42. Scott's	

MAP OF THE ALBANY SETTLEMENT

John and Maria Stanford were in Bowker's party (4) on *S. Weymouth*
Henry and Elizabeth Caroline Warner were in George Smith's party (44) on *S. Stentor*
Joseph Walker was also in George Smith's party (44) on *S. Stentor*
His future wife, **Margaret Booth**, and her parents were in Sephton's party (43) on *S. Aurora*
Edward Driver, was in Calton's party (7) on *S. Albany*.
His wife, **Anne née Thackwray**, was in William Bensted Smith's party (45) on *S. Northampton*.

PEDIGREE TREE OF WALTER ERNEST MORTIMER STANFORD

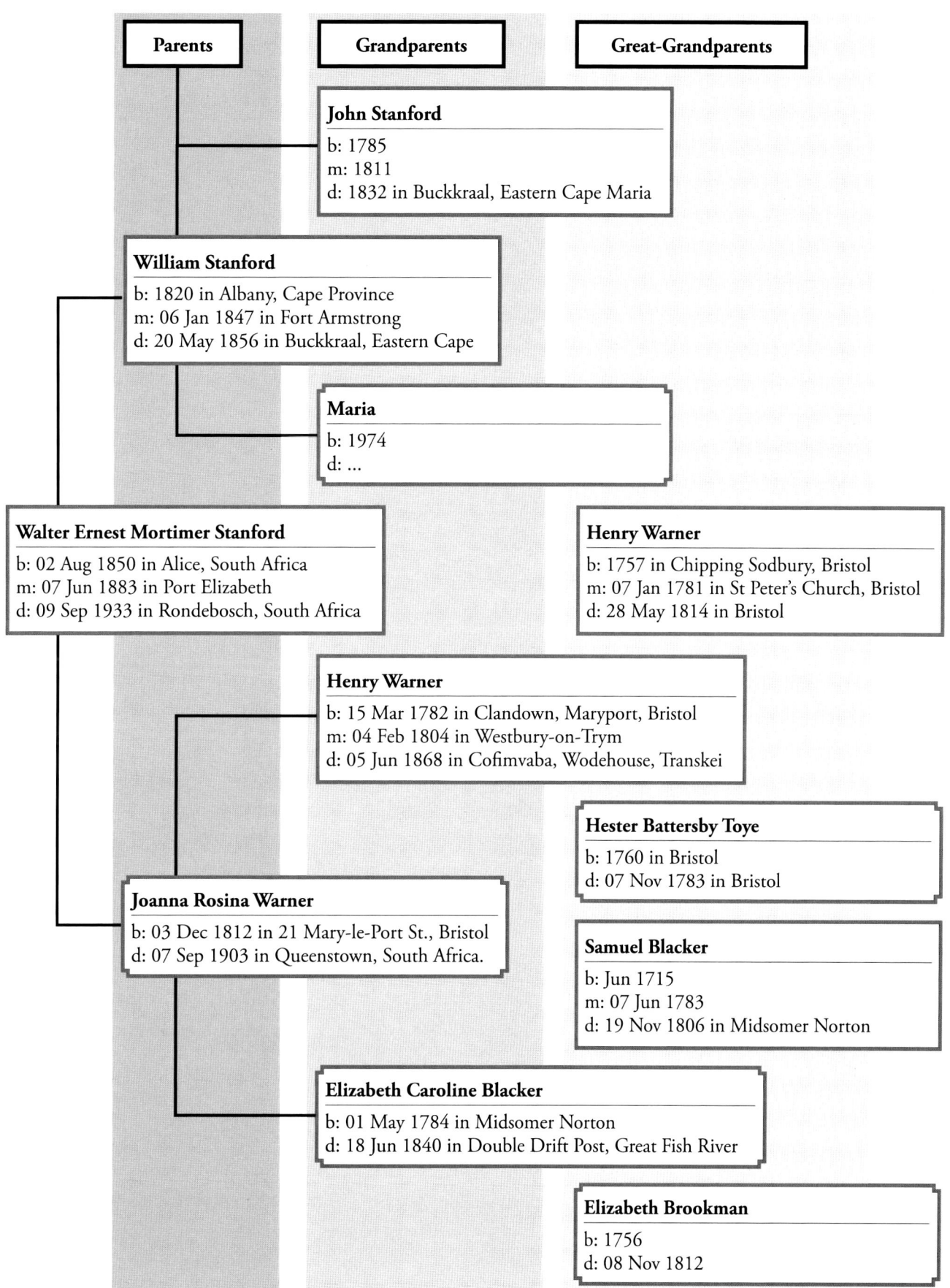

| Parents | Grandparents | Great-Grandparents |

John Stanford
b: 1785
m: 1811
d: 1832 in Buckkraal, Eastern Cape Maria

William Stanford
b: 1820 in Albany, Cape Province
m: 06 Jan 1847 in Fort Armstrong
d: 20 May 1856 in Buckkraal, Eastern Cape

Maria
b: 1974
d: ...

Walter Ernest Mortimer Stanford
b: 02 Aug 1850 in Alice, South Africa
m: 07 Jun 1883 in Port Elizabeth
d: 09 Sep 1933 in Rondebosch, South Africa

Henry Warner
b: 1757 in Chipping Sodbury, Bristol
m: 07 Jan 1781 in St Peter's Church, Bristol
d: 28 May 1814 in Bristol

Henry Warner
b: 15 Mar 1782 in Clandown, Maryport, Bristol
m: 04 Feb 1804 in Westbury-on-Trym
d: 05 Jun 1868 in Cofimvaba, Wodehouse, Transkei

Hester Battersby Toye
b: 1760 in Bristol
d: 07 Nov 1783 in Bristol

Samuel Blacker
b: Jun 1715
m: 07 Jun 1783
d: 19 Nov 1806 in Midsomer Norton

Joanna Rosina Warner
b: 03 Dec 1812 in 21 Mary-le-Port St., Bristol
d: 07 Sep 1903 in Queenstown, South Africa.

Elizabeth Caroline Blacker
b: 01 May 1784 in Midsomer Norton
d: 18 Jun 1840 in Double Drift Post, Great Fish River

Elizabeth Brookman
b: 1756
d: 08 Nov 1812

CHAPTER II

The 1820 Settler Generation

John and Maria Stanford – Walter's paternal grandparents

John and Maria Stanford, from Salisbury, Wiltshire, were 1820 settlers, sailing on the *S. Weymouth* in Miles Bowker's party. Miles Bowker was a gentleman farmer from Manor Farm, South Newton (near Wilton), Wiltshire. He was recommended for settlement by his landlord, Lord Pembroke, who made a personal visit to the Colonial Department on his behalf, and by William Boscowan, a cousin of Lord Falmouth. This was a proprietary party; the eight indentured labourers Bowker engaged to accompany him were all Wiltshire countrymen and, with one exception, single men. The only married man among them was John Stanford, whose deposit was paid by the parish. John was 35 years old at the time, and Maria was 26.

Deposits were paid for nine men: 17-year-old William Bowker, who did not pay the full deposit, was accepted by the authorities as the 10th 'able-bodied man' needed to bring the party to the prescribed minimum size. The journey from South Newton to Portsmouth, where the party was to embark, was made with a borrowed travelling carriage and several farm wagons loaded with household furniture and agricultural implements. The settlers were not able to board the Weymouth immediately, as her fitting up was not yet completed. As a temporary measure, they were accommodated on a hulk, the *Brave*, in Portsmouth Harbour, which was used as tender.

It was bitterly cold, with snow in the air, as the settlers assembled in Portsmouth. The ship's log indicates that most of the settlers went on board on December 16, 1819, and spent a white Christmas on the *Weymouth*. On Christmas Eve, snow began to fall and 569lb of fresh beef and 80lb of vegetables were brought aboard.

Thomas Holden Bowker, one of 12 children on the *Weymouth*, later wrote his own reminiscences of his last days in England:

"After a few days, the time came for our going on board the Weymouth Store Ship, as she was called. She, like our old friend, the Brave, had seen better days and had been a frigate, but had been taken out of the fleet and turned into a transport or troop ship. She was, however, commanded by a set of regular officers and crew, but in a reduced number. She still had a few guns on board and looked like a ship of war. There were already many parties of settlers on board, and others going on board, like ourselves. The Weymouth seemed as large as the old ship we had left, but not so high out of the water, but we were soon all on board where we met a crowd of gentlemen.

"Upon looking about the ship, you might perceive the most incongruous assortment, or utter confusion of articles. The settlers of all classes, high or low, had most of them become travellers for the first time in their lives. They were only beginning to gather by degrees that experience which was wanted to teach them how to pack up things properly and to realise what should have been left behind. Lucky appeared the ordinary class of emigrant who, having only a single chest, could sit upon it at his ease, while those who had larger possessions saw them go down into the hold or saw them piled up, creaking and breaking, to make room for more. But in a short while, all these things were sent down below, except some of the larger articles. My father's long carts were stowed upon the booms before the main mast. The wheels were sent below, as were the artillery wagons.

"The storage of goods completed, the settlers were consigned with their numerous families, amounting to nearly 700 in number, to the small berths in double tiers arranged on each side of the orlop and main decks. The berths were occupied mainly by the women and children; the men slept in hammocks slung in a long row in front of the berths. On the upper deck, the poop cabins were allotted to the more respectable families. On one side was my father's cabin with his eight sons and one daughter, while on the opposite side was a gentleman whose family consisted of one son and nine daughters. A long dining-table reaching the whole length of the poop cabin served for all purposes, and each party occupied their own section."

The *Weymouth* sailed from Portsmouth on January 7, 1820, with all of the party on board, although Bowker's men had already voiced their dissatisfaction with the conditions of their engagement. They declared that they would rather return home as 'poor deluded emigrants than become slaves'. John Stanford was their ringleader, and he was particularly aggrieved to find himself worse off than the parish-assisted emigrants in the party under Samuel James. He considered that he was entitled to receive the full 100 acres of land at the Cape, not the 10 that Bowker was willing to give him. He wrote from the Ship to the Secretary of State for the Colonies, Lord Bathurst, thus:

On Board HM Ship Weymouth

My Lord,

Wishing to state to your Lordship my complaint wherein I find myself very dissatisfied, hoping at the same time for redress from your Lordship. I made a Veritable Agreement with one Mr Bowker to proceed to the Cape of Good Hope not knowing at the same time he was to receive 100 acres of land in my name but his promise to me was ten acres. Now my Lord I have a wife and two children. I am sent out on emigration by the Parish who paid the deposit money. Now I wish to know from your Lordship if I am not entitled to 100 acres of land agreeable to Gov't regulation now Mr Bowker says I shall not have any more than ten acres. There were many familys on board who have been sent out by the Parish and hav the priviledge of 100 acres and why not me the same. I never wish to live with him if he means to defraud me and my family out of what I think in my opinion is just and right however my Lord I am obligated to leave all to your disposal knowing there will be justice done on both sides. I require no more than what is reasonable and just but my Lord I never meant to leave my own Country as a slave nor for my wife and family to be made slaves of. I came in hope of success in my undertakings but success I can expect none if this Agreement stands. I came thinking to derive some advantages of doing good for myself and family not to become a slave this government never meant to be the case. Therefore my Lord I hope you will take this seriously into consideration and give me an answer before I proceed farther on my journey.

I remain with profound respect
Your most obed' humble servant

John Stanford

As the cold of England and the seasickness of the Bay of Biscay were gradually left behind, the settlers acclimatised themselves to life on board, but another problem arose. An outbreak of measles claimed the lives of several children, mostly from the Wiltshire parties, including Sophia and Jane Stanford who died on January 27 and February 10, 1820, respectively.

Interestingly, the *Weymouth* had a rather dramatic encounter during the journey with a Spanish galleon ship that had been hoping to capture what they thought was another pirate ship. The English, of course, also wanted to take possession of the pirate ship. Some shooting took place, which must have scared the poor settlers out of their wits before the Spanish ship eventually sailed away.

On Tuesday, April 25, 1820, Table Mountain was sighted, doubtless to the huge excitement of all on board, and they dropped anchor in Table Bay on April 26. Miles Bowker's wife gave birth to a daughter, Anna Maria while the ship lay at anchor. All the Wiltshire settlers, with the exception of Benjamin Trollip from Hyman's party, continued on to Algoa Bay. The last leg of the journey was to be even more crowded, as two parties of settlers from the *Stentor* transferred to the *Weymouth* in Table Bay and are recorded on the *Weymouth's* muster roll. Amongst them were the Warner family (of whom more later), and Daniel Flinn, who married Maria Stanford after John died.

The ship anchored in Algoa Bay on May 15, but the settlers did not start disembarking for another five days. The Wiltshire parties were discharged on May 23 and settled in Lower Albany. The Bowker party was located on the right bank of the George River. The location was named Olive Burn. By 1823, the party had dispersed, leaving this location to be granted to Miles Bowker himself. M.D. Nash notes in his *Settlers Handbook* that the Ford, Hyman and

1820 Settlers and their Dutch carriers

James parties were "the only settler parties to remain virtually intact under their original leaders during the settlement's first three years".

The following was written by an 1820 settler who did not sail on the *Weymouth*. However, his reaction on arrival at Algoa Bay was doubtless typical of all the Wiltshire settlers.

> "It was a forlorn plight in which we found ourselves when the Dutch wagoners had emptied us and our luggage on to the green-sward and left us sitting on our boxes and bundles under the open firmament of heaven. Our roughly-kind carriers seemed, as they wished us goodbye, to wonder what would become of us. There we were in the wilderness; and when they were gone we had no means of following, had we wished to do so. We must take root and grow, or die where we stood. But we were standing on our own ground, and it was the first time many could say so. This thought roused us to action – the tents were pitched – the night-fires kindled around them to scare away wild beasts, and the life of a settler began."

John and Maria Stanford had six children with them at the start of the voyage to South Africa: Matilda (born in 1810, when Maria was only 16!); John (born in 1812); Laetitia (born in 1815); Jane and Sophia (born in 1818 and 1819, who had died on the journey); and Charles (date of birth unknown). Soon after their arrival in South Africa in 1820, William, who was Walter Ernest Mortimer Stanford's father, was born. Mary, their last child, was born in 1824.

Matilda, their oldest daughter, married Joseph Cox Warner, the brother of Walter's mother, Johanna Rosina. (In other words, brother and sister William and Matilda Stanford married sister and brother, Joanna Rosina and Joseph Cox Warner.) Joseph Cox was to be an important influence in Walter's development.

John Stanford (senior) was given a commission in the newly-formed Rural Police and was stationed near Peddie at Buckkraal, where he died in 1834 aged only 49.

In 1835, his widow, Maria, who had been given the property at Buckkraal, which lay on the Grahamstown side of Peddie, married Daniel Flinn. He was himself a widower, who had come to the Cape on the *Stentor* in Smith's party and transferred in Cape Town to the *Weymouth* for the journey on to Algoa Bay.

DESCENDANTS OF JOHN STANFORD

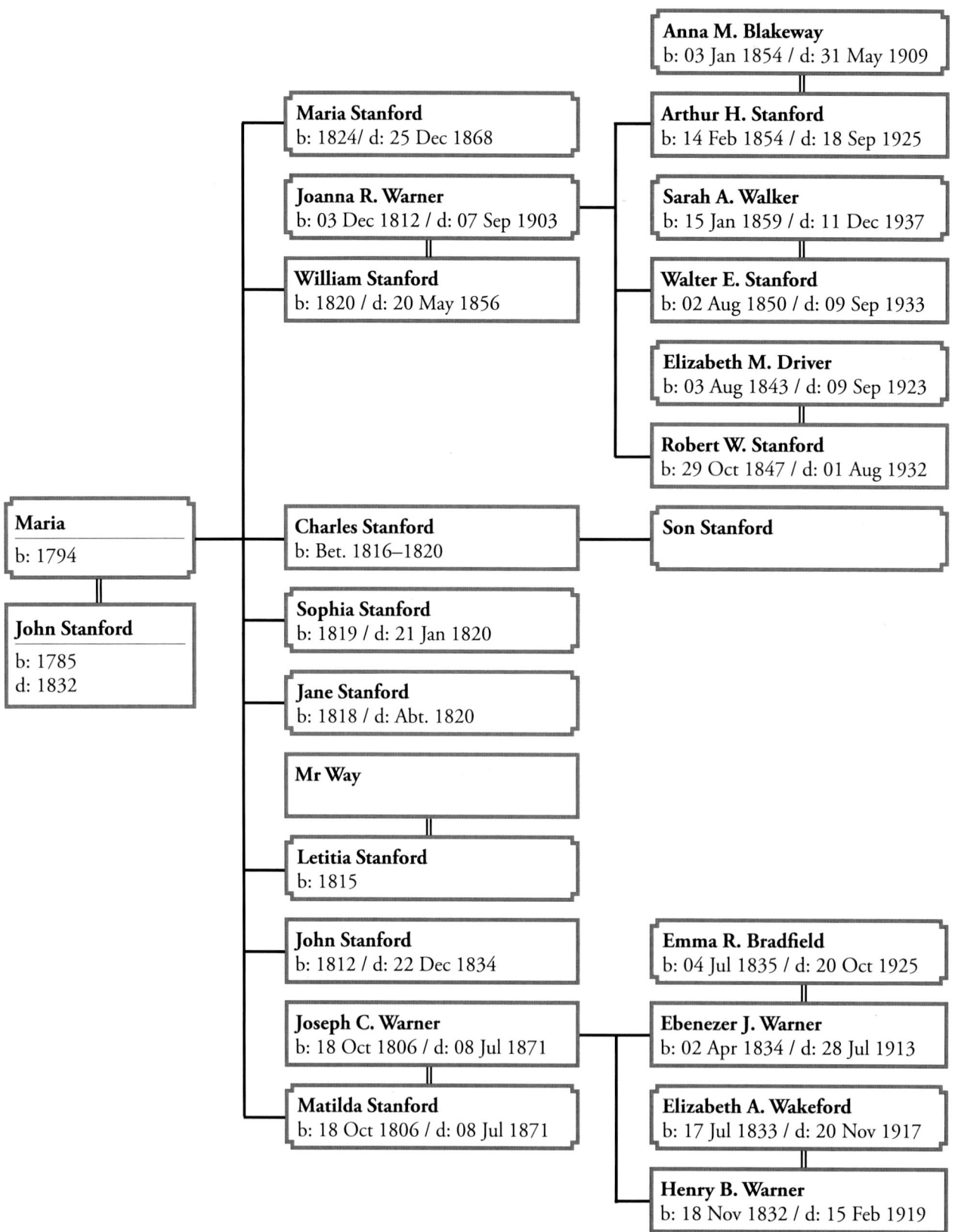

Anna M. Blakeway
b: 03 Jan 1854 / d: 31 May 1909

Maria Stanford
b: 1824/ d: 25 Dec 1868

Arthur H. Stanford
b: 14 Feb 1854 / d: 18 Sep 1925

Joanna R. Warner
b: 03 Dec 1812 / d: 07 Sep 1903

Sarah A. Walker
b: 15 Jan 1859 / d: 11 Dec 1937

William Stanford
b: 1820 / d: 20 May 1856

Walter E. Stanford
b: 02 Aug 1850 / d: 09 Sep 1933

Elizabeth M. Driver
b: 03 Aug 1843 / d: 09 Sep 1923

Robert W. Stanford
b: 29 Oct 1847 / d: 01 Aug 1932

Maria
b: 1794

Charles Stanford
b: Bet. 1816–1820

Son Stanford

John Stanford
b: 1785
d: 1832

Sophia Stanford
b: 1819 / d: 21 Jan 1820

Jane Stanford
b: 1818 / d: Abt. 1820

Mr Way

Letitia Stanford
b: 1815

John Stanford
b: 1812 / d: 22 Dec 1834

Emma R. Bradfield
b: 04 Jul 1835 / d: 20 Oct 1925

Joseph C. Warner
b: 18 Oct 1806 / d: 08 Jul 1871

Ebenezer J. Warner
b: 02 Apr 1834 / d: 28 Jul 1913

Matilda Stanford
b: 18 Oct 1806 / d: 08 Jul 1871

Elizabeth A. Wakeford
b: 17 Jul 1833 / d: 20 Nov 1917

Henry B. Warner
b: 18 Nov 1832 / d: 15 Feb 1919

Henry and Elizabeth Caroline (née Blacker) Warner – Walter's Maternal Grandparents

Henry Warner (jnr) and Elizabeth Caroline (Blacker) emigrated in 1820 in George Smith's party per *S. Stentor*, leaving London at the end of 1819.

Elizabeth Blacker's family was of Clandown, Midsomer Norton, Somerset: the local manor house. Her father, Samuel (born 1715), was prosperous, being a colliery proprietor, a landowner and a farmer. He was also a copyholder under the Duchy of Cornwall. His first wife's name had been Martha, but they had no children. At the age of 68 Samuel married a widow, Elizabeth (née Brookman), who was born in 1756, and they had four children. Elizabeth Caroline was the oldest and was born in 1784. Then came Samuel Palmer (born 1785); Mary (born 1876) and Sarah Patience (born 1880). Samuel (snr) died in 1806 in Midsomer Norton, aged 91. His wife, Elizabeth, died in 1812 aged 56. Samuel left the manor house, as well as a pewter tankard and his liquor barrels to his only son, Samuel Palmer. He also left 600 pounds to each of his daughters. This was eventually inherited (in the case of Elizabeth Caroline) by her daughters. By that time, it amounted to approximately 200 pounds each after deductions for legal charges and interest had been added.

Henry Warner (jnr) was born in Maryport, Bristol in 1782. His parents were Henry Warner (snr) and Hester Battersby (Troye). Henry, senior, was a basket- and brush-maker and Baptist preacher, who was born and lived in Chipping Sodbury until he was about 20. Then he moved to Bristol where he lived in the Castle precincts before moving to 21 Maryport Street. It was from this address that he married his first wife, a young widow, Hester, in 1781. She was the daughter of Joseph and Elizabeth Troye of Maryport Street, and the sister of William Troye, a British judge at Gibraltar. Henry and Hester had two sons, Henry (jnr) and Ebenezer (born 1783).

Family tradition has it that Henry junior and his wife, Elizabeth Caroline, moved from Bristol to Manchester, where their fourth child, Caroline Elizabeth, was born in 1818 because, apparently, he had stood guarantor for a friend who let him down. They therefore moved north in search of employment and a new life. They already had three children: Mary Jane Toye, who was 13; Joseph Cox, who was 12; and Joanna Rosina (Walter's mother), who was five at the time. Times were hard, however, and jobs were difficult to find. So, they decided to emigrate from Britain to the Cape Colony.

They embarked on the *Stentor* and sailed from Liverpool on Wednesday January 12, 1820, arriving at Finchal Road, Madeira, on Sunday February 6, and reaching Table Bay on Wednesday April 19. In Simon's Bay, this party was also transhipped to the store ship *Weymouth* for the rest of the voyage to Algoa Bay, which they reached in May 1820.

Their final destination was New George River (near the Rufane River). This was an area which, even into the 1980s, remained undeveloped and covered with coastal-type bush, which made it look green and fertile, but nevertheless unsuitable for agriculture – particularly the type known and practised in Europe. This location was named George Vale. The eponymous George Smith had been a shopkeeper from Manchester who had served in the British army and been wounded at Waterloo.

Henry was a basket-maker, like his father, and he was a government storekeeper as well as a farmer from 1820–1847. The family left the Grahamstown district in order for Henry to become a missionary (probably in 1835). He was also appointed as a government agent in the Native Territories; so the family moved a number of times. Caroline's younger sister, Elizabeth, was born in Bathurst in 1821, and died there from smallpox when she was only 15. She was buried in the graveyard next to the small church. Henry died in Cofimvaba in June, 1868. Henry's brother, **Ebenezer**, married **Mary Blacker**, his wife's sister.

PEDIGREE TREE OF SARAH ALICE STANFORD (NÉE WALKER)

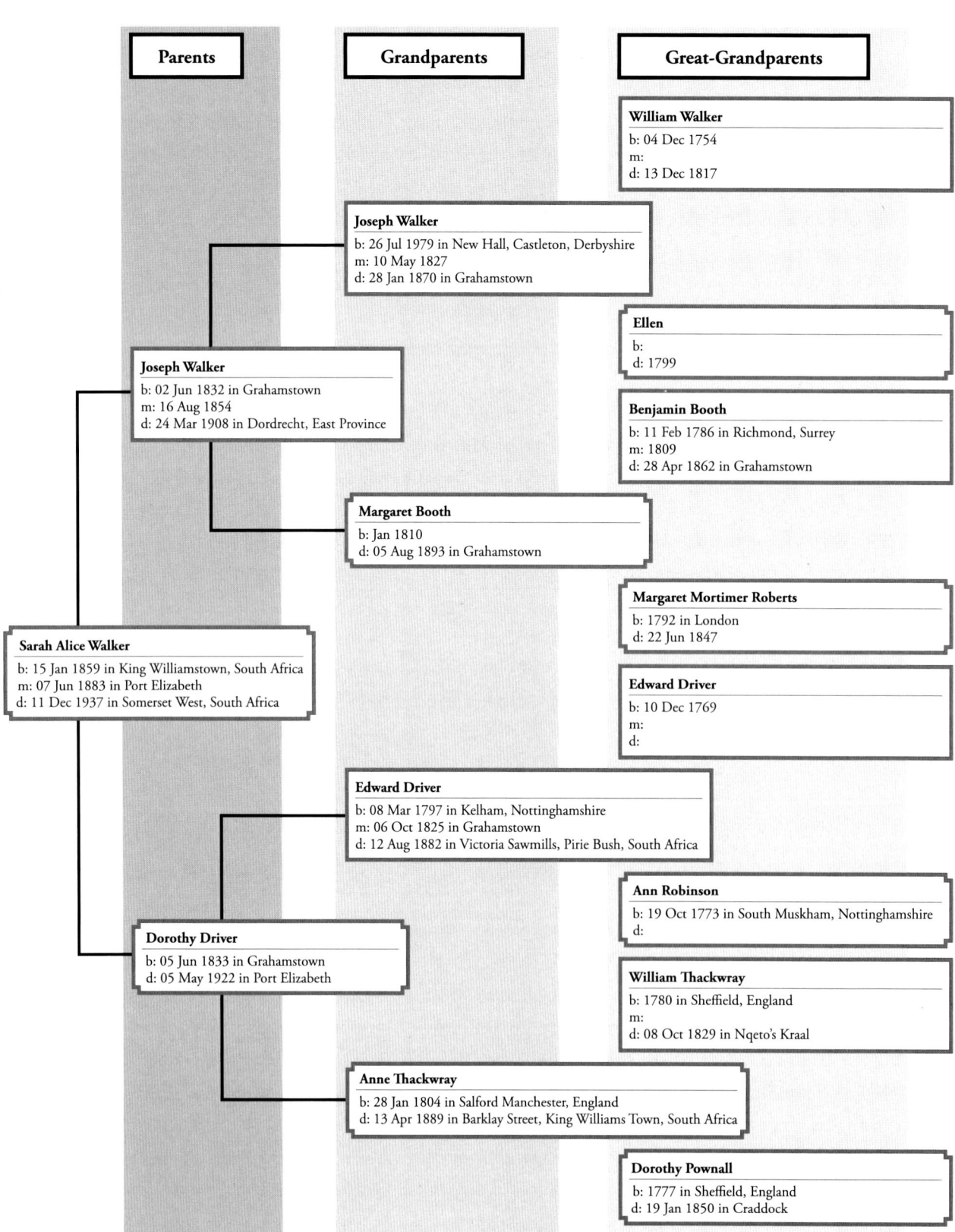

Parents	Grandparents	Great-Grandparents
		William Walker b: 04 Dec 1754 m: d: 13 Dec 1817
	Joseph Walker b: 26 Jul 1979 in New Hall, Castleton, Derbyshire m: 10 May 1827 d: 28 Jan 1870 in Grahamstown	
		Ellen b: d: 1799
Joseph Walker b: 02 Jun 1832 in Grahamstown m: 16 Aug 1854 d: 24 Mar 1908 in Dordrecht, East Province		**Benjamin Booth** b: 11 Feb 1786 in Richmond, Surrey m: 1809 d: 28 Apr 1862 in Grahamstown
	Margaret Booth b: Jan 1810 d: 05 Aug 1893 in Grahamstown	
		Margaret Mortimer Roberts b: 1792 in London d: 22 Jun 1847
Sarah Alice Walker b: 15 Jan 1859 in King Williamstown, South Africa m: 07 Jun 1883 in Port Elizabeth d: 11 Dec 1937 in Somerset West, South Africa		**Edward Driver** b: 10 Dec 1769 m: d:
	Edward Driver b: 08 Mar 1797 in Kelham, Nottinghamshire m: 06 Oct 1825 in Grahamstown d: 12 Aug 1882 in Victoria Sawmills, Pirie Bush, South Africa	
		Ann Robinson b: 19 Oct 1773 in South Muskham, Nottinghamshire d:
Dorothy Driver b: 05 Jun 1833 in Grahamstown d: 05 May 1922 in Port Elizabeth		**William Thackwray** b: 1780 in Sheffield, England m: d: 08 Oct 1829 in Nqeto's Kraal
	Anne Thackwray b: 28 Jan 1804 in Salford Manchester, England d: 13 Apr 1889 in Barklay Street, King Williams Town, South Africa	
		Dorothy Pownall b: 1777 in Sheffield, England d: 19 Jan 1850 in Craddock

Joseph and Margaret (née Booth) Walker – Alice's paternal grandparents

Sarah Alice (née Walker)'s paternal grandparents were also 1820 settlers. **Joseph Walker (snr)**, (her paternal grandfather), born in 1797, came from a large family in Castleton in the Derbyshire Peak District. He was the eighth child of his mother, Ellen, although two had died in infancy. In 1799, Ellen had another daughter, Margaret, but sadly she and the baby died, leaving her husband, William, to raise his family alone. William died in 1817, when Joseph was 20. Joseph and his brother Richard were energetic young men and ready for adventure. They joined Lt George Smith's party, setting sail on the *Stentor* on January 12, 1820, from Liverpool, and arriving in the Cape on April 19. Richard was already married to Martha (née Littlewood) with a small son, also Joseph, and a baby daughter, Elizabeth.

The *Stentor* was ultimately bound for India, and therefore unable to complete the journey to Algoa Bay, so the brothers also had to transfer to the *Weymouth* for the last stage of the journey. The ship anchored in Algoa Bay on May 15, where George Smith, the leader, was allowed ashore. Everyone else had to wait until onshore accommodation became available. They were finally allowed to disembark on May 22. They were settled east of what is now Port Alfred and had no choice but to start clearing the land with a view to farming. Neither of them had any experience as farmers!

Joseph Walker (snr)

Joseph quickly set about acquiring more land, including 300 acres at George Vale, and two farms on the Kowie River. At that point he felt able to marry and found a young bride, 17-year-old Margaret Booth, from among the other settler families.

Benjamin Booth (snr)

Margaret (née Booth), was born in 1810 and emigrated with her parents, **Benjamin** and **Margaret**, and her two sisters, Sarah and Jane, in Sephton's party aboard the *S. Aurora*. This was one of the largest parties, with 101 men and 66 families, split between the *S. Aurora* and the *S. Brilliant*, with a surgeon accompanying each party, along with a young Wesleyan minister, Rev William Shaw. The two ships sailed relatively late in the scheme, having been held up by bad weather and only leaving Gravesend on February 15.

The Booths, staunch Methodists, came from London and were settled at Salem. Later, the Booth family moved to Reedfontein, south-west of Port Alfred. Benjamin and Margaret had a son, Benjamin, in September 1820, and three more daughters, Elizabeth, Mary and

Emma. After his wife's death in 1847, Benjamin (snr) moved into Bathurst Street in Graham's Town (later Grahamstown) to be near his daughter and son-in-law, Margaret and Joseph Walker. In 1854, Benjamin, aged 68, married again, to a widow, Grace Brent (née Elliott). He died in Bathurst Street in 1862. From his photo, Benjamin looks to have a twinkle in his eye and a friendly face. There are some examples of little wooden dolls he made for his children in the Albany Museum.

Joseph Walker and Margaret married in Graham's Town, and by 1828 were living there. Joseph became the owner of a store in Bathurst Street, and continued to trade for the rest of his life. He also steadily accumulated more land and eventually became a prosperous businessman and citizen of Grahamstown. His store grew from a simple enterprise that sold the necessities of life into a thriving business that imported and sold a wide range of luxuries: "Fineries of Every Description with Family Mourning, Meal, Coffee, Sugar, etc.". He became a shareholder in the new Eastern Province Bank, although some of his investments were not that successful. Joseph and his brother, Richard, were both pillars of the Wesleyan community and had strong faiths. They both became involved in supporting charities and doing good works.

Three generations of Walkers, circa 1867. Joseph (snr) seated centre, with his grandson, Joseph Benjamin, beside him. From left to right: Benjamin (his 2nd son); William (his 4th son); Rev W.G. Holford (married to his 2nd daughter, Ellen); Joseph (jnr) (his 1st son). Joseph Benjamin was Sarah Alice's brother and the next in age to her.

Joseph and Margaret had 11 children between 1828 and 1848. The oldest son, Joseph (jnr) was the father of Sarah Alice. Joseph Walker (snr) died in 1870 and is commemorated by a plaque in the Commemoration Church in Grahamstown. Margaret died 23 years later, also in Grahamstown.

Edward and Anne (née Thackwray) Driver – Sarah Alice's Maternal Grandparents

Edward Driver

Edward Driver and his wife, Anne (née Thackwray), were both 1820 settlers, but married after their arrival in the Cape Colony. Edward was born in 1794 and came from Kelham in Nottinghamshire. According to David Walker in his book *Pawns in a Larger Game*:

> "Young Edward was intelligent, sharp, well set-up, and quick with his fists. He liked to think of himself as cock of the walk and was well pleased with his nickname of Kelham Ned. He was one of many young people who could see little future in Nottingham."

He emigrated as part of Calton's party on *S. Albany*, and his occupation was listed as "grocer". His grandson said: "My grandfather, Edward Driver, came out with the 1820 settlers, paying all of his own expenses; a fact which he always related with pride." The party were settled northeast of Bathurst, where Edward began his life as an agriculturist, eking out a living by tilling virgin land. He became a hunter, guide, fighter and trader and a captain in the Albany Sharpshooters 1834/5. Some of his military escapades were heroic, and some rather more questionable.

As a young man, he was apparently not beyond a bit of sharp trading (if not illegal!), and he found himself in many scrapes. In 1821, he became embroiled in an argument with one William Sykes. No love was lost between the two of them, and Sykes was drunk. Edward was aggressive and Sykes, furious. Sykes eventually fired his gun at Edward who fell, wounded. Edward was peppered with shot. He was treated in Grahamstown, where the pellets were removed and he recovered quickly.

In 1835 he was wounded at Murray's Krantz during the sixth Frontier War. After the Seventh Frontier War, he moved his family to Peddie, and became a foundation member of that Divisional Council. He bought plots in the village at the first sale in June 1849. It is interesting to note that in 1850, Edward gathered his entire family to be baptised before the Peddie Methodist Minister. Perhaps this was a sign that the reprobate had finally found respectability! In 1854, he bought titles of the farms Gwanga and Willow Park. He died at the house of his daughter, Mrs Hannah Haynes, in 1882.

Edward and Anne married in Grahamstown in October 1825, and Anne gave birth to their first daughter, also Anne, only five months later. It must have been an awkward conversation that Edward had with his prospective father-in-law! The couple eventually had 12 children: The fifth of whom, Dorothy (born in 1833), was Alice Stanford's mother.

Anne was the daughter of **William Thackwray** (born in 1780), of Sheffield. He was an agricultural implement maker who had initially enlisted with Baillie's party. However, he withdrew from that party to join William Bensted Smith, who promised him and his son, John, 100 acres of land. William Thackwray's wife was **Dorothy Pownell**, from Bath, England. She was three years older than her husband. They sailed from London aboard the *S. Northampton*. By December 1820, William Thackwray and his family were encamped at Algoa Bay. It was there that he appears to have taken as an apprentice, a young lad, **George Wood**, who had escaped from an unkind master who had threatened to send him back to England.

Mary Bell, great-granddaughter of George and Susan Wood, wrote in her book *They Came from a Far Land:*

"The first we hear of George Wood after his escape from the ship (*S. Aurora*) was when he appeared before the magistrate in December 1820 to be apprenticed to a Grahamstown wagon-maker named Thackwray. Possibly Thackwray, who was encamped with his family at Algoa Bay when the Aurora arrived, took him into service then, for George could hardly have got away from there by himself. John Thackwray, the 18-year-old son, a kind-hearted lad who became George's closest friend, may have come upon the stranded boy and taken him to his father for help. All we actually know is that George Wood worked for William Thackwray as an apprentice.

"So did Thomas Stubbs, who was 11 at the time. 'Old Thackwray was a strange sort of man. He was very strict, and from his talk would be taken for a Quaker as he always said yea and nay and thou.' Meantime, George Wood's mother was inquiring about him, as she had had no contact from him. She received a letter in 1822 written by a bureaucrat, River, and forwarded to her by Lord Bathurst, saying that George's indentures 'are dated 5 November 1819 and were formally transferred or assigned on December 6, 1820, by the mutual consent of the Master and apprentice in the presence of a Magistrate, to W. Thackwray, a wheelwright and carpenter residing in Graham's Town, with whom the boy now lives. I informed the lad that his mother had made inquiries respecting him, and he assured me that he would write to her, which he said he had not done since his arrival in the Colony. He is in good health and learning a trade under a respectable Master.'

"The settlers were forbidden, on pain of death, to trade with the Xhosas but, rather than see their families starve, the dangerous and illicit trade went on. One of the traders was John Thackwray, (William's son) a slight, good-tempered young man who seems to have been attracted to danger. George Wood's apprenticeship to the elder Thackwray had not lasted long. Young Wood may have downed tools and walked out – he was that kind of lad. But why should his Master, to whom the indentures gave a cheap servant for six years, allow him to go? The law would have brought him back.

"According to later gossip, Wood was seen leading oxen, barefoot in Grahamstown streets. Stubbs says that he led ox wagons for traders into Xhosa territory. Since it was about this time that young Thackwray took to trading, the

Hon George Wood, prosperous in his later years

chances are that young Wood led John Thackwray's oxen, and that an anxious father had released a difficult apprentice so that his son might have a companion to help him on his hazardous trips.

"Henry Dugmore, a settler who later became a missionary, describes the hazards: The stealthy crossing of the border, the appointed meeting-place beyond it, the life-in-hand venture into the power of the Xhosas, the perilous return when dark nights and difficult ways had to be selected, and quick-sighted patrols of mounted riflemen dodged in the bush paths.

"Neither Thackwray nor Wood were daunted by hardship or dangers, but John Thackwray had no flair for business and was one of the few who could not make trading pay. The two young men had to part, though they remained firm friends. John Thackwray went elephant hunting, and in 1828 was in fact killed by an elephant. Wood, who had not taste for hunting, but had a very real business flair, went on leading other men's oxen, and later driving their wagons, 'til he could afford to buy a wagon and trade for himself."

Eventually, through trading and buying property, the Honourable George Wood became a very wealthy man and an influential politician of those times. On his death, he left an estate valued at over £264 000!

William and Dorothy Thackwray settled eventually at Stoneyvale, to the east of Grahamstown. William Thackwray was murdered in 1829, aged 49, by Chief Nqueto, together with Lt Farewell and William Walker (no relation), en route to Natal at Nqueto's Place. Edward Driver (his son-in-law, married to his daughter, Anne) had refused to accompany them and warned them against going there, as he did not trust Nqueto. Edward died in Pirie Bush in 1882.

Some of Anne Driver's wearing apparel was preserved, according to her wishes, so that later generations could see how they dressed. Members of the family have some, and there is a frock donated by the family in the Albany Museum, Grahamstown. Anne was buried in King Williams Town in 1889.

One of Anne Driver's frocks in the Albany Museum, donated by the family.

CHAPTER III

The First Generation Born in South Africa

William and Joanna Rosina (née Warner) Stanford – Walter's parents

William Stanford was born in 1820, soon after his parents, John and Maria, landed in Algoa Bay. William served in the Rural Police and later in the Frontier Armed Mounted Police, with the rank of captain. His marriage to **Joanna Rosina Warner** in Fort Armstrong in 1847 was officiated by the Rev William Ritchie Thomson, and the couple first lived in Alice, Eastern Province.

The family moved to Buckkraal, near Peddi, when William became a member of the St Victoria Mounted Police. The couple had three children, Robert William (born October 1847), Walter Ernest Mortimer (born August 1850) and Arthur Henry Bell (born February 1854). Walter had some dim recollections of his father, although he was only six when William died. According to my grandmother, Dorothy, William was said to be a fine rider and loved 'a good horse', but in May 1856 his horse ran away with him and galloped into the stable, crushing William's leg. It had to be amputated and he died shortly afterwards. He was buried in the Fort Beaufort cemetery.

Joanna Rosina Warner was born in 1812 in Bristol and emigrated with her family. Their party was transferred to the *Weymouth* for the final part of their journey, where the Warner family and the Stanford family would first have met. However, in 1830, Joanna Rosina married William Wright and they had three children, William, Mary and Rosina. William Wright snr came out at age 20 in Neave's party, on the *Stentor*. On reaching Cape Town, this party was first located on the left bank of the Zonderend River, in the Caledon district. Shortly thereafter, most of them were moved to Albany to join the other settler parties. Joseph Neave, himself, remained in the Caledon district. William Wright jnr became the first Chief Magistrate of Tembuland. When William Wright snr died in about 1839, his widow, Joanna Rosina, and her children spent some years residing with her father, Henry, or brother, Joseph Cox, at their mission stations.

In 1847, she married William Stanford, and a traditional family story, which has come down by word-of-mouth through the Wright family, claims that Joanna Rosina used to say: "I married William Wright for security, but I married William Stanford for love." However, members of the Stanford family have always wondered why she waited so long before marrying William Stanford. They claim he pressed his suit for some years before being accepted. Perhaps the age difference had something to do with the delay (she was eight years his senior).

After William Stanford's death in 1856, she resided with her brother, Joseph Cox Warner, for some years. Her sister, Mary, who was slightly disabled, assisted her with the boys' early education. Walter described his mother as a small woman of indomitable courage who continued trading, farming and transport-riding while still finding time to encourage her sons to read and write. A small person of great character!

In *Stanford's Reminiscences*, Walter tells an anecdote that illustrates his mother's sense of fairness and moral courage. On about his third day of formal schooling at Lovedale, aged about 10, he was subjected to a punishment for nine mistakes in a dictation: The strike rate being 20 cuts per mistake!

Joanna Rosina Stanford (Stanford's mother)

"The master, Mr Ross, used a light sjambok. He did not strike hard, but constant practice had given him great skill, and he imparted a good deal of sting into what might appear to be light taps. My native companions at Glen Grey had taught me that it was manly to bear pain without flinching, so when my turn for punishment came I held out my hand and Mr Ross administered 100 cuts before he stopped.

"On my arrival home that afternoon, I said nothing to my dear old mother of what had happened, but the next morning at breakfast, she noticed that I could not use my right hand. It was much swollen and I had then to explain how this had come about. My mother was not a woman to submit quietly to what she thought was an act of grave injustice, so she went to the school with me and had an interview with Mr Govan, the headmaster.

"Mr Govan was evidently shocked when he heard the story and saw the state of my hand. I believe Mr Ross got the wigging he certainly deserved."

The government granted her a farm at Buckkraal in recognition of William's service. She lived with her faculties unimpaired to the age of 91 and died in Queenstown in 1903. A beautiful leaded light pane window was erected in her memory in the Anglican Church in Queenstown, where it can be seen to this day, on the left-hand side, towards the altar.

Joseph Cox Warner, who was Rosina's oldest brother, played an important role in Walter's formative years, and was a great influence on him, so I include here his story!

William Stanford's oldest sister, **Matilda** (Walter's paternal aunt), married Joseph Cox Warner (his maternal uncle). When Walter's father, William, died, as we have already seen, his mother, Rosina, and her six children went to live with Joseph and Matilda Warner, where Matilda's youngest sister, Mary also lived. It would appear that Walter himself was sent at first on his own to live with them. He says in his memoires:

"My health having been seriously broken down, arrangements were made for me to be taken by wagon to Glen Grey, in the hope that the change up-country might be the means of saving my life… My welcome at Glen Grey was a warm one, and soon I was able to move about and play with the native boys who were the only companions available. Glen Grey was a seat of administration and a mission station combined. Mr Warner had been pressed by Sir George Cathcart to accept the office of Tambookie Agent. He had done so reluctantly, having been previously engaged in mission work. Umtirara, the Paramount Chief of the Tembu tribe, who had great confidence in Mr Warner, feeling his end approaching, had sent for him. As a dying request, he had asked him to take care of his children and tribe. This no doubt weighed with Mr Warner in accepting the appointment offered to him by His Excellency the governor."

Walter also relates an anecdote that demonstrates the principles by which this couple ran the mission.

"I remember too the arrival at Mr Warner's house of a native man with his wife and child seeking work. They had suffered from the famine and were kindly received and given aid by Mrs Warner, whose kindness to the native people has lived long in their memories. The name of the man was Jantje Gcali of the Tembu tribe. He remained on the mission, proving to be a man of sterling character. He learnt to read and write and by steady consistent work and good Christian conduct was eventually ordained as a minister in the Wesleyan church."

According to his grandson, C.J. Warner:

"Joseph Cox Warner arrived in the Cape Colony at the age of 14 years, and when he attained manhood he first had some notion of entering the Mission Field among the Native tribes of the Cape, and lived for some years at the Mission Station of Mt. Arthur, where his second son, Ebenezer, was born (in 1834). J.C. Warner became acquainted with Ngubengeuka, the Paramount Chief of the Great Tembu tribe, and acquired great influence over him and his tribe. Because of his Christian character and sterling good qualities, the Tembus had the utmost trust and confidence in him, and when in later years (1852) the Governor of the Cape Colony wished to appoint a resident with Ngubeneuka, the Tembus would only consent to the Governor's request on condition that J.C. Warner would be the resident."

While at the Wesleyan Mission in New Bristol between 1820 and 1835, Joseph Cox worked with Shepstone to translate the scriptures into Xhosa. J.C. Warner is also credited with being instrumental in making peace with the invading Fecani army and in setting up of a mission station amongst them. He and Matilda enthusiastically set about their work, even though they endured many hardships and, at times, danger. When Joseph rode out to meet the Fecani army to try to persuade them to return captive women and children, his fellow missionary, who had taken a gun, against his wishes, fired it to frighten the Fecani. They immediately set upon him, stabbing him to death. The unarmed Joseph narrowly escaped with his life. Matters only took a turn for the better when Joseph found a wounded Fecani warrior after a subsequent attack on the mission station. He nursed the warrior back to health and returned him to his chief unharmed.

J.C. Warner continued in his efforts to bring about peace between the tribes and to protect their lands from the Dutch settlers, the Boers. In 1846, he was influential in preventing the Tembu tribe from getting involved in the 'Kaffir Wars'. However, when the governor, Henry Smith, under pressure from the Boers, declared all of Tembuland to be British territory, Joseph was left to appease the natives, as they were all effectively being punished for their involvement in the war – even the Tembu.

As the Boers continued their unprovoked attacks, accusing him of being a 'rebel', Joseph was forced to evacuate the region, leaving behind most of his belongings. However, by 1852, with his name cleared, and by then appointed as the government officer in charge of the Tembu tribes, he began locating them into reservations; maintaining peace between them and the white farmers; encouraging Christianity and 'industrious habits'. He was considered such an expert in 'Kaffir' laws and customs that he was asked to write a compendium for use by government officers. By the time he retired from his post in the late 1860s, some natives had their own small farms within the reservation.

In his book, *An introduction to South African Methodists*, Prof Lesley Hewson writes:

"Among those who later manned the pioneer stations were some who stand in the great tradition of men who made themselves one with their people, speaking their language, knowing their customs, entering into their sufferings and hardships, rebuking their evildoing, sheltering their outcasts and championing their interest. Among these will be remembered J.C. Warner who came to be called the uncrowned king of the Tembu."

Hewson also writes of the work done by the early missionaries in the studies and use of the Xhosa language:

"William Shaw is the first, but, in this company, not the greatest name, for after him came W.B. Boyce with his collaborators Theophilus Shepstone and J.C. Warner… Boyce was responsible for the so-called 'Euphonic concord', which enabled him to understand the elements of Xhosa grammar, but Eveleigh quotes a tradition that 'Boyce ploughed with Warner's heifer'."

After some time, Joseph Cox was appointed British Resident for the Transkei and Tembuland, and took up his abode at Cofimvaba. He retired on pension some time before 1870, and went to live on his farm at Glen Grey. In 1871, he was the founder and first member of the Queenstown Assembly, having defeated Sir Gordon Sprigg in the first election. (Sir Gordon Sprigg later became Prime Minister of the Cape.) Joseph Cox was also elected Member of Parliament for the division of Queenstown. In the same year, while travelling by postcart from Queenstown to Port Elizabeth to take the steamer for Cape Town in order to attend the session of Parliament, he took ill on the journey, had to leave the postcart at a place called Balfour, at the foot of the Katberg Mountain, and died there after a brief illness.

Joseph and Dorothy (née Driver) Walker – Sarah Alice Stanford's parents

Joseph Walker (jnr) was born in Grahamstown in 1832 and married **Dorothy Driver** in 1854, after a relatively long courtship of two years. He lived first in King Williamstown and was a partner in a firm of merchants – Maynard, Walker & Co, who traded in East London and King Williams Town. In his book, A.D.M. Walker writes: "At the end of 1866 Joseph and his partners were embarking on a major litigation case in the Supreme Court, suing Richard Southey in his capacity as a Colonial Secretary, for unpaid debt by the Colonial Government. They alleged that a cargo of hoop iron, carried by a Government vessel, had been negligently destroyed. The sum involved was about £80, which does not sound serious but compared with average earnings at the time it was equivalent to almost £50 000, a not insignificant sum. The case was to drag on for a considerable time with no resolution."

Later he was to suffer further business setbacks and moved to Port Elizabeth. Politically, he was a supporter of the Progressives led by Cecil Rhodes and represented Dordrecht as a Member of the Legislative Assembly in Cape Town for nine years. He lived in Hamilton House, Port Elizabeth, and died in 1908. Dorothy is said to have kept in touch with her descendants and never lost her broad and sympathetic outlook. She, too, spent her last years living in Hamilton House, Port Elizabeth, and died there in 1922.

Joseph Walker jnr,
1832 to 1908
and
Dorothy née Driver,
1833 to 1922

Dorothy in later life (photograph courtesy of A.D.M. Walker)

CHAPTER IV

The Second Generation Born in South Africa

Robert and Arthur Stanford – Walter's brothers

Walter's oldest brother, **Robert William**, was born in Fort William in 1847. We know little of Robert's early years. He did not go to live with Joseph Cox Warner and his wife, Matilda, nor, I think did he go to Lovedale College. Wherever he was educated, he was clearly successful in his chosen career which, like those of his brothers, was in the Civil Service. He rose to be Assistant Chief Magistrate in the Transkeian Territories and was stationed at Kokstad by 1902. During his career he held several Assistant Magistrate positions. In the *Reminiscences*, Walter writes:

> "Mr Thompson's health gave way and at his own request he was brought back to the Transkei, being succeeded by my elder brother, R.W. Stanford, who later was appointed Assistant Chief Magistrate for Eastern Pondoland under Major Elliot."

He was also courageous and a leader. Walter mentions several incidents in which Robert played a leading and active role.

> "Mr Levy and his people were rescued by a force sent in from the Tambookie Location under the command of Mr R.W. Stanford.

> "Several hundred cattle driven off by the enemy on our advance were captured by Commandant R.W. Stanford, who had moved up from St Mark's with the native levies."

Robert William Stanford as a young man

He displayed skill as a diplomat and emissary on other occasions. Walter tells of one such incident:

"Le Fleur (he was Andrew Abraham Stockenstrom Le Fleur, a Griqua chief) then with his following, about 50 men, fled towards Pondoland through the district of Mount Frere. Mr R.W. Stanford, Assistant Chief Magistrate for Pondoland East, was advised of his flight towards Pondoland. He at once sent for Sigcawu to whom it had become known that Le Fleur had sent messengers previous to the outbreak. Mr Stanford informed him of Le Fleur's flight in the direction of Pondoland East and of his seditious action in East Griqualand and pointed out to Sigcawu that, if Le Fleur were not promptly arrested on his arrival, such inaction, coupled with the fact that the messengers had been received by Sigcawu, would certainly implicate him as supporting Le Fleur in his rebellious designs. The result of the interview was that Sigcawu had Le Fleur arrested at once on his reaching Pondoland, and delivered him to the authorities. At his second trial Le Fleur was convicted of sedition and sentenced to 13 years' imprisonment with hard labour. On receipt of news of his apprehension, I was at my office in Cape Town and my clerk, Mr J.B. Moffat, thought the occasion worthy of celebration at the Civil Service Club. I agreed."

On another occasion, he again displayed a sense of moral integrity and courage. Walter wrote:

"A coldness had arisen between my good old friend Elliot and Rhodes, when he visited Fingoland and pressed the introduction of the Council system. Elliot was opposed to the tax upon the Fingos being fixed at 10 shillings a man. He advised five shillings, and in this connection wrote a report which was dealt with by Sprigg (Sir Gordon) in Cape Town during Rhodes's absence. An official letter, personally signed by Sprigg, was written to Elliot unfairly criticising his report. This caused umbrage, not only to Elliot himself, but to his magistrates as well. Accordingly, a deputation headed by R.W. Stanford saw Rhodes and entered their protest against what had been done to their chief. Rhodes replied that had he been in Cape Town, the letter of which they complained could not have been written, but he added that Sprigg was a colleague of his and further than that statement, he could not go."

However, this seems not to have diminished the respect with which Robert was held by those in power, and specifically by Sir Gordon Sprigg himself, who became prime minister. Walter describes his own appointment as Chief Magistrate of the Transkeian Territories thus:

"Before he left, (1902) the Prime Minister (Sir Gordon Sprigg) consulted Major Sir Henry Elliot regarding the future administration of native affairs in the Transkeian Territories as a whole. In reply, Sir Henry recommended the consolidation of the Territories under one chief magistrate and added to Sir Gordon Sprigg that in his opinion, my services should be requisitioned as the first Chief Magistrate of the Combined Territories. This involved the retirement of Mr J.H. Scott who had succeeded me as Chief Magistrate of East Griqualand in 1897. Sir Gordon accepted the advice and asked me if I would be willing to go back to the Territories; it being understood that the able Assistant Secretary to the Native Affairs Department, Mr W.G. Cumming, should succeed me as permanent head of the department.

Sir Gordon Sprigg

"To this change I raised one objection. It was that my younger brother, Mr A.H. Stanford, was Assistant Chief Magistrate to Sir Henry Elliot at Umtata, and my elder brother, Mr R.W. Stanford, was Assistant Chief Magistrate at Kokstad for East Griqualand, and that this conjunction of the three highest public offices in the Transkeian Territories would certainly be adversely commented on in some quarters. Sir Gordon Sprigg's reply was that he knew all three of us and had no doubt whatever that in any matters dealt with, each of us could be relied upon simply to do his duty."

In 1874, Robert married Elizabeth Maud Driver in Queenstown. Maud, as she was known, was the younger sister of Dorothy Driver who, when Maud was only 11, had married Joseph Walker and was the mother of Sarah Alice Walker. Robert and Maud Stanford had three children; Maude Driver (born in 1879); William Harry Driver (born in 1881); and Claud (born in 1883). This marriage was another complicated linking of the settler families. Robert's brother, Walter, was married to his wife's niece!

Robert William Stanford

Robert's great niece, Sheila Kilpin (née Stanford) described him thus: "He was a magistrate in the Transkei. I remember him living in Kokstad. They had a big house in Hope Street and a big black carriage. He was a fierce man of whom we were frightened. I didn't know Aunt Maud, but we once stayed with him and his daughter, Maudie, when Mom and Dad went somewhere. Maudie was a very good cook, (as in Maudie cake). Poor Maudie. Uncle Bob chased away any young man who came near her, and she never married." Robert died in Port St Johns in 1932 – a year before his brother, Walter. Maud died 11 years later in Kokstad.

Arthur Henry Bell Stanford was Walter's younger brother. He was born in Alice in the Cape in February 1854 and was educated in Alice and Fort Beaufort. After experimenting with farming, the diamond diggings and the law in 1875 at the age of 21, he joined the public service of the Colony and became a clerk to Mr William Wright, the British Resident in Tembuland. William Wright was Arthur's older half-brother, first son of Joanna Rosina and her first husband, also William Wright.

Ngangelizwe, Paramount Chief of the Territory, was beset by enemies on every side and sought the protection of the British Government. His country was annexed to the Colony, and Mr Wright became the first Chief Magistrate. Young Arthur's outstanding ability and devotion to duty won the admiration of his superior officers, and he was quickly promoted.

In September 1878, at only 24, Arthur Stanford became a Resident Magistrate.

In June 1880, he married Anna Maria Blakeway whose father was a magistrate in Umtata. They had six children: Mabel Beatrice Annie, born in 1881; Etheline Myra Louise, born in 1882; Alan Arthur, born in 1884; Harold Reginald, born in 1887; Mary Charlotte, born in 1892; and John, born in 1893.

By 1880, Arthur was the Magistrate in Umtata.

Walter mentions an incident there:

> "The following morning (October 25), the Pondomisi collected in some numbers, being joined by Pondos as well, and traders' stores in Pondoland near to Umtata were looted. The house occupied by the Magistrate of Umtata, Mr A.H. Stanford, a little way out of the town on the west bank of the river, and the homesteads of farmers in the vicinity, were dismantled."

He became the Assistant Chief Magistrate in Umtata in 1902, and later the Chief Magistrate of Transkeian Territories. He clearly did his work conscientiously, as Walter comments: "At Umtata, the Assistant Chief Magistrate, Mr A.H. Stanford, had kept the work well up to date."

Arthur, known for his administrative and judicial ability, was a prominent freemason and a member of the Church of England. The regard in which he was held by senior political figures in the Cape Colony is demonstrated by the anecdote quoted by Walter about his

Umtata Town Hall in 1910, as Arthur would have known it.

appointment in 1902 (see notes about Robert William Stanford above). The long obituary that appeared a few months after his death in the *South African Law Journal* gives a full account of his career and draws a picture of a retiring, but intensely effective administrator and upholder of the law:

"On the 18th September, 1925, there passed away at Umtata Arthur Henry Bell Stanford, for many years Chief Magistrate of the Transkeian Territories. Although, whenever he could do so, he preferred to keep out of the limelight of public affairs and thus was not well known beyond the circle of his own friends and those with whom his duties had brought him in contact; it is nevertheless true that in him, South Africa lost one of her greatest Native Administrators and one of her ablest exponents of native law and customs.

Born in 1854, Arthur Stanford on both his father's and mother's side came of the stock of the British Settlers of 1820. He was educated at Alice and Fort Beaufort. After experimenting with various openings for a career – including farming, the diamond diggings and the law – his course in life was settled once and for all when in 1875, at the age of 21, he joined the public service of the Colony and became clerk to Mr Wright, the British Resident in Tembuland. Ngangelizwe, Paramount Chief of that Territory, beset by enemies on every side, had sought the effective protection of the British Government. His country was annexed to the Colony and Mr Wright became the first Chief Magistrate. Young Arthur's outstanding ability and devotion to duty quickly won the approbation of his superior officers and it was not long before he began to climb the ladder of promotion, for those were the days when splendid opportunities opened out before able young men.

In September, 1878, while still but 24, Arthur Stanford became Resident Magistrate of the recently established district of Umtata. In 1885 he was transferred to the important district of Engcobo, where he remained till 1894 when, upon the annexation of Pondoland, he was selected to be the first Magistrate of the district of Libode in West

Pondoland, where the Paramount Chief of that Territory had his "Great Place." Three years later he was back again in his old district of Umtata, and in October, 1897, was appointed Assistant Chief Magistrate of Tembuland and the Transkei.

In 1907 he became Chief Magistrate of the Transkeian Territories with jurisdiction extending from the Kei to Natal and from the coast inland to the Drakensberg. This office Mr Stanford continued to fill until his retirement at the age of 60 in 1914. The late General Botha, in a personal letter, urged him to undertake a further term of office, but considerations of health and a desire not to impede the promotion of his subordinates induced him to decline the invitation.

After his retirement he paid his first and only visit to England, a visit which unfortunately was cut short by the outbreak of the Great War. The closing years of his life were spent in the little cathedral city on the Umtata River which was the headquarters of the administration over which he had so ably presided. He took an active part in its civic life – for he was a model citizen – and did much to advance its welfare, especially in connection with the hospital for which he had always worked devotedly.

Major Sir Henry Elliot, Chief Magistrate of Tembuland from 1877 to 1891 and of the combined territories of Tembuland and the Transkei from 1891 to 1902, well and truly laid the foundations of the Transkeian system of Native Administration, and from 1897 on, he was finely supported by his assistant, Arthur Stanford. When the latter took over the reins of the whole Territories in 1907, he did so not only with a complete equipment of judicial and administrative experience, but with the advantage of being already well known to and trusted by the natives. He had an incomparable way of winning their confidence and esteem, and it was this characteristic more than any other that enabled him to lift the Transkeian Territories General Council, over which he presided from 1905 to the date of his retirement, to the unique and outstanding position it has won in the native administrative systems of South Africa. This is not the place to speak of the constructive work accomplished by the General Council under his wise guidance. What is perhaps even more important is that during his presidency he established, among the Native Councillors, a tradition of moderate speech and dignified behaviour which reflected his own conduct of its proceedings, and which correspondingly added to the weight of the Council's deliberations. He worked not only for the tranquillity but, in an even greater degree, for the progress of the tribes under his control, believing that with their moral and economic advancement the incentives to disturbance would disappear.

As a lawyer, Mr Stanford possessed in an eminent degree not only the legal, but the judicial mind, an especially valuable combination in the peculiar circumstances in which he was called upon to preside over the Native Appeal Court. For when taken over by the British Government, the law of the native people was still developing on its own lines. Contact of the people with European law was also bound to result in curious reactions to their own law. It was essential that these tendencies should be wisely guided without the law being rendered vague and uncertain, and it is due to Mr Stanford's judicial capacity and the administrative experience that a due measure of elasticity was preserved. Viewed thus, his work as President of the Native Appeal Court was perhaps even more valuable than that of the administrator.

As a man, Mr Stanford was – but how can one who knew and esteemed him for what he was, speak of his qualities! And the writer is but one of the many trained in his school of public duty and efficiency who knew and esteemed him. Firm he was always. Stern he could be when any dereliction of duty called for sternness. If he promised it was only when he could fulfil, it was against his straightforward nature to raise false hopes in European or Native. His intimate friends were not many; the privilege of being one was the more to be valued. He was of a fine and commanding presence; he had the gifts of a quiet eloquence, a clear delivery, a peculiarly melodious enunciation. Perhaps the most charming of his traits was a simple uprightness of character coupled with the modesty that so often accompanies high qualities.

He left to those who come after him a great example and a great tradition."

Walter received this letter following his brother Arthur's death:

"Dear Sir Walter,

On Saturday evening I received the sad news that my dear old Chief Mr Arthur Stanford had passed away. My heart is sore and, as far as one not a relation may do so, I mourn with you most sincerely. Therefore, I hope I may be allowed to express my deep sympathy with you and your family in your sorrow and loss. Mr Arthur Stanford was to me almost like a father. I recall with feelings of deep gratitude the many occasions on which he by kindly advice and the utmost consideration helped me in the course of my official work in the days when it was my good fortune to serve under him. Since then I have always valued very highly his friendship and esteem and was much disappointed that I did not see him on the occasion of my last visit to Umtata. I had lately heard with much sorrow of his failing health. His death is a great loss to the Country.

The patience, tact, and ability with which he guided and controlled the General Council through the most awkward stage of its existence always struck me as entitling him to a place in the first rank of Native Administrators and the wonderful success of the Council system, about which one hears so much nowadays, is undoubtedly to be attributed in no small measure to his great gifts in the government of Native people. To you and to him. I owe much, and therefore hope you will not think it out of place that I should make mention of the fact in this letter of condolence.

With kind regards,

Yours very sincerely,
Newton O. Thompson

Walter Ernest Mortimer Stanford with his brothers, Arthur (seated) and Robert

CHAPTER V

Walter Ernest Mortimer Stanford

In telling Walter's story, I have quoted extensively from the Introduction to the two volumes of his *Reminiscences*, published by the Van Riebeck Society and edited by J.W. Macquarrie, which gives a summary of that career. From 1848, as Macquarrie states:

"Step by step, African territory between the Fish River and the Natal border was annexed, and European magistrates and police were sent in to rule. Between the years 1858 and 1894 the boundaries of the Cape were extended from the Kei River to the Natal border, and the non-European population increased, from about 200 000 to not far short of 2 000 000, largely as a direct consequence.

This extension of responsibility, unsought and unwelcome, particularly in its earliest stages, was not achieved without bloodshed. The tribes encountered were warlike and independent. The cost to the Europeans, however, was trifling for many reasons; among which was that almost as many Africans supported the Europeans as fought against them. On the African side, the losses, too, were not great, and possibly less numerous than they would have been if the intertribal warfare endemic to their mode of life had continued during this period.

When these territories, later to form what is now known as the Transkei, were taken over, their peaceful development was ensured by a Native Policy that took cognizance, on the one hand, of European ideals of justice and equity, and on the other, of native law and custom. Thus, from the outset it was a 'unique progressive policy adapting itself to the various stages of advancing civilisation. The Transkeian administrators', according to Brookes, 'pursued a defined course, and Transkeian policy presents itself as a coherent, intelligible, progressive and conscious evolution'.

Credit for this policy of peaceful development was attributable not to the ministers in 'far-off Cape Town', except in so far as they 'had the good sense to leave men who knew something about their subject a free hand in policy… Everyone knows that the Transkeian experiment has succeeded, as far as Europeans are concerned, owing purely and simply to the permanent staff of the Native Affairs Department, and particularly to the Resident Magistrates, and in particular to Charles Brownlee, Matthew Blyth, Henry Elliot and Walter Stanford'.

The uniqueness of Stanford's contribution is that, in effect, it covers the whole period of transition. He began in 1863 as a clerk to the Tambookie Agent just within the borders of the semi-independent native territories. He took an active and a leading role in both of the campaigns that led to the incorporation of these territories, and in the much more difficult and delicate work of pacification that followed the campaigns. His public career ended in 1929, when he was representing in the senate the interests and aspirations of the populations of these territories. By that date, they had formed an integral and inseparable section of the State."

Born in 1850 and only six when his father died, Walter Ernest Mortimer was sent soon after to live with his uncle, Mr Joseph Cox Warner, at Glen Grey in the Queenstown district (later to be known as Lady Frere). His mother took this decision in the hope that the higher altitude might improve his poor health. According to a family account, Walter was dosed with turpentine, or some equally strong fluid, when he was very young,

The Lovedale Missionary Institution

and thereby his digestion was seriously, and to some extent permanently, impaired. That his health was completely restored is amply proved by the long and strenuous career that followed. Mr Warner, as we know, led a busy life.

Walter spent the next three years with Mr Warner and received some schooling from a maiden aunt, Miss Mary Stanford. He then rejoined his mother, who had gone to live in Alice, and for the next two years, 1860–1861, he was educated at the Lovedale Missionary Institution. There, his fellow pupils were bright, Xhosa-speaking indigenous lads, who were receiving an education in the missionary tradition. This, Walter's only formal education, terminated before he was 12 years old, although it has been said that while stationed at Glen Grey he continued his interrupted education by riding to Queenstown every weekend to study with Mr Beswick, the principal of the public school.

On July 1, 1863, just before his 13th birthday, he became a clerk under his uncle, Joseph Cox Warner, at Glen Grey, and so entered the service of the Department of Native Affairs. He would remain there for about 45 years. There, he was destined to exercise a profound influence on the development of South Africa.

Responsibility came early. He was barely 13 years old when, during his uncle's temporary absence, he became, in effect, Tambookie Agent – Her Majesty's representative in a semi-independent African tribe. On October 21, 1869, after six years of employment at £60 per annum, "the country", he drily noted, "could no longer afford to retain my service." For several months, he was employed in private business as a bookkeeper, and then returned to the Department of Native Affairs at the greatly enhanced salary of £120 per annum. The next few years were spent mainly in Queenstown and East London. In his *Reminiscences*, he provided a short but vivid account of these towns and some of their leading personalities in the early 70s.

Walter as a young man

Walter advanced steadily in the Civil Service. In April 1876, aged 26, he was appointed Magistrate with Dalasile, chief of the AmaQwati tribe. In the so-called Ninth Kaffir War, the Gcalekaland Campaign, Stanford was commissioned and placed in charge of a division of native levies. In August 1877, he wrote from Encgobo to his mother about an expedition he had undertaken with his brother, Arthur:

2 August 1877

My dear Mother,

I had arranged with Arthur last week that we should go out shooting on Monday to one of the large forests in the neighbourhood, but much to our disappointment we had to give up the little trip we intended to have made for shooting purposes. On the Saturday, I got an express from Mr Whitmore, the field cornet at Sleng River, telling me that Mr North, the mining engineer at Soon Kop was coming to the upper part of this district to examine coal formations which had been discovered there, and that he wished if possible that I should meet him. I arranged to do so accordingly, and on the Monday which we intended to have been our first day at the Buck hunting, I had to go off coal hunting instead.

The place at which we were to have met was the "Juhansea" one of the sources of the Bashu, and near the northern boundary of the district. On arriving there we could hear nothing of Mr North nor of Mr Whitmore, the discoverer of the coal. So at sundown, I rode to the Moravian Mission station at Entemanazand, which is a few miles beyond, and Mr Hasting together with his wife made me very welcome and comfortable for the night. The next morning, a letter came from Mr Whitmore telling me that Mr North had been prevented from coming and that Mr Dunn would come instead. I waited at Mr Hasting's until afternoon and then Mr Whitmore arrived alone, saying Mr Dunn had come as far a Juhansea but could not manage time to get to the upper Bashu where the more important coal discovery had been made, so he had gone back. I began to feel much "exercised" about the whole affair. Fortunately, I had not thought it necessary to wait about all the morning but had gone out with my gun and had a good look at the country round. Entemanazand lies about 10 miles from the farm of Brackensberg, and there had been a fall of snow a day or so previously on the hills, so that the top part of the mountains was still white. The mission station is in a valley and after climbing up to the ridges, I was able to get a great view of the Drackensberg and the country stretching towards Umaitshwa location on the one side and Dordrecht way the other. The hole in the rock was visible, and about 12 miles on the Dordrecht side of the spot where I was standing.

Nine years before I had been near the ground I stood on – what changes had taken place since then – I hardly like to think of some of them. It makes one fear the future. But I found Nature a shade older. The fantastic outlines of the hills brought to recollection my first impressions of them, and the singular shapes presented by those mountains can only be seen to be realised.

It surely must have been here they fell after the giants "hurled them at their enemies in days of old." Mass rises on mass and the effect of that day was heightened by the white of the snow above the klaafs, which run deep into the sides of the mountains, making the heights above appear overhanging and about to plunge into the depths of the valleys below.

But, to return to our "coals" – Mr Whitmore and I started off on the following morning for the upper Bashu, which was really on my way home, for although at one of the sources of that river it is not one that runs up to the Drackensburg, I had first to go a little out of our way to examine a bit of land that has long been a "bone of contention" between two petty tribes up there. So, it was about four o'clock in the afternoon when we reached the "coal". It had been discovered in a most extraordinary place. The country is comparatively level from the front of the Drackensburg to the summits of the Zuanberg or Jalanhada ranges. At the base of the higher line of rocks forming the brow of the latter rand and at the same time the southern limit of the plain I have mentioned the seam of coal has shown itself. It is about two feet in thickness, and from specimens examined by people competent to judge and say it is good. I think the seam runs along the whole extent of the rocks, which here form an elbow of about two to three miles long. At the angle so formed is the celebrated (in these parts) Bashu waterfall. The stream of water is very small, unfortunately. Standing where one cannot see the bottom of the fall, the water vanishes amongst trees which line the sides of its course like sentinels guarding its beauties from vulgar eyes, and they do it efficiently too. We had an unpleasant scramble down the hill and found ourselves getting late. However, I pushed on and managed to get home at half past 10 last night pretty well tired and with a low opinion of coal hunting and mining engineers generally. Today, I felt all right again and have done a good day's work after my 13-hour ride yesterday. Especially considering that today is my birthday and I am 27. Getting old. I have lately realised, too, that Arthur is grown up. The important facts to get hold of: We did not have a row to arrive at our relative positions (The last sentence is illegible)

Goodbye with love
 Your affectionate son
  Walter

That he was a brave and resourceful officer is borne out by a despatch from the commanding officer, Major (later, Sir) Henry Elliot, dated November 28, 1877, and reading "Captain Walter E. Stanford, commanding No. 1 Division, upon every occasion displayed great gallantry, energy and judgement; his Division being generally used as advance guard, came into more contact with the enemy than any other did. I cannot speak too highly of his conduct."

In March 1878 he wrote to his mother from Camp Huka Drift:

My dear Mother,

I must send you a line to tell you that our expedition against Slakwe Lyali and Umfando has been a great success. My division had most of the fighting to do and we managed to punish the enemy pretty well, but at some loss to ourselves.

One of our volunteers, a brave young Dutchman named Nicholas Gessinger, was killed, and three natives were also killed and five wounded, so we suffered more severely than we usually do in these engagements. This was owing to the fearfully rugged nature of the country. "Maxongis Hack" which we had to attack is a long klaaf in the Drakensberg. The stream rising in it is one of the sources of the Bashu. Immense rocks and precipices are on all sides, and deep ravines as well. Such trailing and climbing I never saw even in the worst parts of Falukaland.

We captured a great deal of stock, which was nearly all stolen the same night from our people. The latter were splendid animals, the pick of the Upper Districts no doubt. A system of thieving has been carried on in these fashions for years.

Many thanks for your letters of the 18th. I received the day before yesterday. Reading with me has become quite out of the question. There is something attractive in this life — one moment stillness, idle with nothing to do — the next all life bustle and excitement. But I shall be glad to get back to my quiet and peaceful occupations.

At the conclusion of the war in 1878, he returned to his civil duties at Engcobo, but peace was short-lived. In the same year, Sprigg, the Prime Minister of the Cape, secured the passing of his Peace Preservation Act; more commonly and more appositely referred to as the Disarmament Act. It caused considerable resentment among the native population, and misgivings among administrators such as Walter, who saw that the measure would weaken the loyal and obedient tribes more effectively than the disloyal and disobedient.

In 1880, when Sprigg enforced the disarmament of the Basuto, the Basuto chiefs actively opposed him, and rebellion spilled over the Drakensberg into the Territories. Hope, the magistrate of Qumbu, was murdered on October 23, and four days later Stanford was forced, under cover of darkness, to evacuate the residency at Engcobo. With his staff, both native and European, and with the few Europeans who had remained in the area, he was able to reach Dordrecht safely. In the light of the atrocities committed by so-called civilised nations in the two recent World Wars, it is chastening to read in Walter's account of the chivalry of tribal African chiefs towards the women and children of their enemies.

Map of Engcobo and Clarkebury area

In November 1880, Walter wrote to his mother, describing his escape with others from Engcobo:

Dordrecht
1 Nov 1880

My dear Mother

I sent you a telegram from the Indwe to tell you I had safely arrived that far on Thursday. Friday we were busy assisting the "loyals" in Cumming's district to get out and Saturday evening we reached this place.

I hardly know where or how to begin an account of my escape from Engcobo. For some time previously, it had been evident that secret communication was carried on between the chiefs, but no one anticipated so sudden an outbreak. On Monday, I knew that it was coming and sent word to the traders to leave the district. Those who did so at once were not molested, but others who delayed, suffered for it.

On Tuesday I took Mimmie & Minnie* in a cart I had purchased to Clarkebury. Poor Minnie was still so weak that I delayed sending them off as long as I could. I packed a buck wagon with things, but much was left behind. In fact, nearly everything belonging to me, and Mimmie's piano and other property. Mr Hargreaves (Rev P. Hargreaves who later was in Pondoland) provided us with a cottage, and the wagon with five cows I sent with it reached Clarkebury Tuesday evening.

On Wednesday I had to leave early and started about seven. I went to Enfamazana to see Major Boyes and found him just 'trekking'. From there, I came over the mountain to Engcobo. All appeared quiet. The people ploughing and very few congregated at Dalasile's kraal. I had been fortifying Engcobo and hoped to have a good garrison of white men and "loyals" to defend it.

On my arrival I received information that I was to be attacked that night, and on numbering my attacking force I found there were nine white men and about half a dozen natives. There was nothing for it but flight, and there came the question: Which way? The whole country in this direction was unsettled, and the roads to Clarkebury and Fingoland were blocked that afternoon. It was a case of shut in. One or two might have made a race for it to Clarkebury, but I had the wife of a trader with me, besides the nine Europeans and a handful of natives. After careful consideration I decided to try to crack Dordrecht or Barkly. The men coming out with me assembled at the office at sundown all ready. I broke all the guns we could not bring with us and the ammunition was thrown into water. Of my things I could only take just a few in my pack bags. The last article I took out of the house & put in the Pack bags was your portrait. Before sundown the Inatis were looting Sutton's shop at All Saints on one side and T's at Engcobo drift on the other, and my movements were being watched. I waited until dark, having sent my cattle towards Fingoland as a blind, and then we left the old place for – well – none of us knew where. I took one of my hunting tracks as being the least frequented. Our party were Danniel, Sutton, C. Kuher, Kuher, A. Moore, D. Short, F. Lewis, J. Twill, Willard, No,O. Webb, Mrs Willard and myself, whites excepting Mrs Willard by the way who is coloured. And Jamjam with six of her natives.

I "formed" my little troop about half a mile up the road towards the bush and told them the difficulties before us pointing out the necessity of obeying my orders and above all that we should "stick together". There did not appear much chance for us then. I took the road over the mountain travelling rather slowly on account of Mrs Willard and avoiding every kraal. The foxhounds followed and seemed to know by their silence and their neglecting to hunt that something was wrong. We rode steadily along the mountain ridge until we struck the wagon road. Halfway to Mr Cumming's place, I halted for a rest, but ordered saddles and bridles to remain on the horses. I was aware that all my people were in arms in this direction as well as the other, and we had to be careful not to raise an alarm. Having a woman with us was a great cause of anxiety. After about ten minutes' rest we went on again and in passing a deserted shop the hounds broke away and attacked a skunk. Delighted as I am generally to hear their "music" on this occasion I thought it terribly discordant and I went for those hounds. Fortunately, they came in at once when I called them, and their barking although to my ears loud enough to have roused the whole country, attracted no attention. By this time Mrs Willard, who is a heavy woman, could get her horse no farther. We put her on another I had and pushed on again. On reaching the border of Mr Cummings' district we perceived two strong lights on our right steadily burning and grass fires were spoken of, but it soon became evident they were shops burning. So just when we began to think we had escaped our hopes were dashed to the ground and we were approaching a thickly populated part of the country.

We entered Cummings' district about two or three in the morning and carefully avoided every kraal. Here my knowledge of the country and that of my men was very useful. We marched all night without rousing even the dogs at a single kraal. Just before daylight we reached the Tsomo drift. We could see a light in Mr Cummings house and all were overjoyed to think we were near the end of our ride. But I observed the light flickered strangely and after watching it I came to the conclusion that figures were passing and repassing before it or else it was being carried from room to room. Either Cumming was "packing" or else the rebels were looting his place. We approached cautiously and I sent forward a scout to ascertain how matters were. The light disappeared as soon as we were near enough for our horses tramp to be heard. My scout could make nothing be heard at the house and Mr Danniel & old Webb went forward. They knocked at the doors and there was no response. Then we knew that Cumming had gone and that we must prepare for hot work, as daylight was just appearing and we should be seen. The disappointment was great and at no time during our long and trying ride did we all feel so depressed as then. We marched on to the ridge overlooking Cummings' ridge and off-saddled. After about 15 minutes a head cautiously appeared over the ridge. We took no notice and finally one of Gecelo's men armed, showed himself fully before us. He entered into conversation and told us Cumming had left for the Mbokotwe Mission Station the previous day on seeing the shop looted before his eyes.

For some time, he would not come close to us, but finally got friendly. The sun had risen and the enemy's scouts began to move about on the hills, so we moved on.

Our informant had said we should meet Cumming at Kennedy's so we took the direct road, leaving the mission station to the right. Opposite it we saw men moving towards us rather fast, and they charged towards us on the top of a ridge, taking ground on our right. I think they found our party stronger than they anticipated and when they appeared about to fire I asked what they meant.

They did not answer, but turned off a little way. I called out and asked where the magistrate was. One fellow whose face I recognised said he was just leaving the mission station for Kennedy's. We went on and got near Kennedy's without further molestation and were delighted, as you may suppose, to meet George Dugmore and the relief party with him. Shortly afterwards Cumming turned up with his men and we realised at last we were saved.

Mr Dugmore deserves great praise for the gallant way in which, with so few men, he came to our rescue. I have told you already how we came in from Kennedy's

I am now busy organising forces for the border of this division and hope to be on the way back to Kafirland the day after to-morrow. I would like much, very much, to run down and see you all, but matters here are badly managed and I feel it my duty to remain and do all I can to get them better. Perhaps after a week or two I shall be able to get away.

You can imagine my meeting with Cumming at Kennedy's. We had both been passing through the fire.

The people here have been very kind to us all. Some of the sawyers and traders with their families have been plundered of all they had, and are now receiving rations from Govt. A subscription list for them was started today and we have enough to achieve their present necessities.

I could fill sheets with the stories of their sufferings and their escapes, but after all considering how completely we all were in the midst of our foes very few lives have been lost.

All of our party I think felt gratitude to Providence in their hearts when at last we found ourselves amongst friends.

I am anxious about poor old J and her children. I started them off in the afternoon in my little wagon, but before I left, I heard they had been stopped.

I have been busy all day & now it is late at night. I cannot manage to write a letter for Bob. Send this on to him with my love, and with love to all of you in Queenstown, and the Bolotwa as well

Your affectionate son,
Walter

*Mimmie was Mrs Chabaud (née Wright), Walter's half-sister; Minnie was her daughter.

At Dordrecht, under the authority of the Secretary for Native Affairs, the Hon William Ayliff, Walter Stanford and William Gordon Cumming, the Magistrate of Xalanga, were authorised to enrol volunteers from among local Europeans and loyal Africans. Among the units so formed was a mounted body that was named the Wodehouse Border Rovers. It comprised two troops. Stanford was given command of B Troop.

The rovers participated in the relief of Maclear on December 6, 1880, and in the battles, skirmishes, and mopping-up operations against the rebels along the slopes of the Drakensberg.

In 1881, he returned once more to magisterial work, which involved the difficult task of relocating the defeated chiefs and their tribesmen, and the still more delicate and perplexing negotiations with European squatters in the area. The correspondence published in the *Report of the Tembuland Commission* testifies to the fairness of the permanent officials, the magistrates, and to the tenacity which they displayed when attempting to ensure that their native charges were justly treated.

The Native Laws and Customs Commission. BACK LEFT TO RIGHT: *E. Glanville, T. Shepstone, Dunbe[1], Toto1, Tyuka[1], Rev J. Chalmers.* FRONT LEFT TO RIGHT: *W.L. Stanford, J. Ayliff, Sir Jacob Barry, Sir Thomas Upington, Dr James Stewart, J. Noble.* [1]*Native witnesses*

Alice Stanford (née Walker) and Walter Stanford at the time of their marriage

In March of the same year, he had to attend in Grahamstown the first meeting of the Native Laws and Customs Commission, to which, as a young man, barely 30 years old, he had been appointed.

In 1883, Walter married Alice (Sarah Alice Walker) in Port Elizabeth. Their first son, Walter Elliot (referred to as Elliot to avoid confusion!), was born in 1884. In 1885, Walter was appointed Chief Magistrate of Griqualand East, with headquarters in Kokstad.

There is no doubt that there was real affection between Walter and Alice, and he had a gentle teasing quality when writing to her:

Engcobo, August 19 1884

"My dearest old wife,

As I wrote to you only yesterday I am not sure that I shall be able to find much to tell you. To tell you that I still miss my little wife everyday is to tell you what you know very well, and for which I expect you are not sorry when you write to me sometimes and say how dull you are without me. I take comfort in thinking rather that than not to be missed.

Goodbye my dear old girlie.
Best love, kisses for you.
Your loving husband
Walter

The move to Kokstad brought him into direct touch with Pondoland, a territory which, peopled with a bold and indeed turbulent tribe, was the sole remaining independent native area between the expanding states of the Cape and Natal. It is little cause for surprise, therefore, that its affairs should have been Stanford's chief preoccupation over the next troubled decade. Stock thefts, intertribal intrigues and animosities, concession-hunters, German agents, and even the conflicting interests of the Cape and Natal, caused continual anxiety in Stanford as administrative head of the contiguous territory.

In a memorandum he notes: 'Things were pretty tense at times. Scaremongers were busy, rumours of war frequent, and many hours did I spend unravelling the true from the false in the strange reports which reached me. My own native police would bring me information regarding raids and stock thefts, and half an hour later a wild white trader fleeing as if for his life would bring a strangely contradictory tale.'

According to MacQuarrie: "Tension grew throughout 1886. The Pondos executed several cattle-stealing raids upon the Xesibes and Bacas, and there was friction between the Pondos and the Cape Government regarding the extension of British sovereignty over Mount Ayliff and Port St Johns, and the Cape's desire to purchase the Rode. Realising the need for a display of power, on November 5, 1886, the government authorised Stanford to muster a force of some 200 Cape Mounted Riflemen and 2 300 native troops, under Col Bayly on the Pondon-Xesibe border.

"Walter Stanford was also empowered to send, on the same day, an ultimatum to Umqikela, the paramount chief of the Pondos, which referred to his hostile acts and called upon him to give within four days 'such offer of reparation and proposals for the future control of your people, as you may wish to make'.

Adam Kok, founder of Kokstad (photograph from the Stanford Collection at the University of Cape Town)

"Umqikelo expressed his willingness to negotiate, and at the conclusion of a series of meetings between his representatives and the Chief Magistrate, from December 7–10, 1886, a treaty was signed. By this treaty, the Pondos agreed: 'to open the road from Port St Johns to Kokstad and allow construction, repairs, and outspan places wherever necessary; to establish in conjunction with the Chief Magistrate of Griqualand East a better system on the border; and to carry out, especially in cases of theft, the provisions of their own laws with regard to the punishment of thieves and the restoration of stolen property, or compensation for it'. The purchase of the Rode, which lay across the wagon route from the Cape to Natal, was also satisfactorily arranged."

Just as they were shaping towards a satisfactory conclusion, Walter claims the negotiations were almost wrecked by Prime Minister Sir Gordon Sprigg. He relates that on December 7, in the middle of the negotiations, he received a telegram from Sir Gordon instructing him to break off the talks and to leave Pondoland immediately. Walter replied diplomatically, asking for an extra day, but, as he said: "we were a good many miles away from the nearest post office, and the express rider was not urged to speed." This telegram, as Stanford observes, was not included in the relevant Blue Book. (The Annual Blue Book was a key item of considerable standing in 19th century colonial administration, containing accounts of the Civil Establishment, of the Colonial Revenue and Expenditure, and of various statistical particulars.)

Chief Magistrates' group, Kokstad (front row, second from left): Walter Ernest Mortimer Stanford

On December 9, 1886, the same day that the treaty was signed, Walter and Alice's second child and first daughter, Dorothy Maud, was born in Kokstad. It is likely, therefore, that Alice was not able to have her husband on hand during her confinement!

Macquarrie states:

"In October 1887, Paramount Chief Umqikela died, and having no son by his great wife Masarili, a daughter of Kreli, he left no recognised heir. He was succeeded by one of his inferior sons, Sigcawu, (or Sigcau), who had great difficulty in establishing the authority due to him as a paramount chief. The memoirs describe events leading up to the decision of Rhodes and his Cabinet to annex Pondoland – if possible by negotiation, and failing that, by force of arms."

Before these negotiations took place in 1894, Walter and Alice had three more children. Robert Cecil was born in 1889, but sadly died at age two in 1891. His older brother, Walter Elliot (Uncle Elliot), remembered his father sitting at the bedside of Robert Cecil, holding his hand through his illness and death as a result of diphtheria. Apparently, Robert kept telling everyone to give the things they were offering him to "the baby", his little sister, Alice Minnie, who was born in 1890. Arthur Warner was the next born in 1893.

Throughout the 1880s there was continued trouble and cattle stealing between the Xasibes of Mount Ayliff district and the Bacas. A decision was made to establish a line of farms along the border, which were to be owned by white farmers who were expected to keep the peace between the tribes. In about 1890, Walter bought three farms together: Inungi, Alwyns Poort and Engelo. The boundary on the border side was a strong fence: District Fence Number Three. This was put up by the government in the early 1900s in an attempt to stop the movement of cattle during the rinderpest epidemic, which was introduced from the north by trek spans and the trade of cattle from areas where this disease was endemic.

In March 1894, Major Elliot was entrusted by the government with the duty of conducting the negotiations to take over Pondoland. Accompanied by Stanford and a few personal attendants, but without an escort of troops, he arranged a meeting; first with Sigcawu, nominally the Paramount Chief of all Pondoland, but in effect, the Chief of Eastern Pondoland only.

Elliot, as Stanford records, delivered the government's ultimatum bluntly, but not without understanding and sympathy. Not unnaturally, Sigcawu asked for some time to confer with his chiefs and councillors on the matter. Elliot gave him 10 days, until March 19, and moved on to meet Nqwiliso, the Chief of Western Pondoland, leaving Stanford to conduct negotiations with Sigcawu.

From Walter's own account, it would appear that the sole reason why Sigcawu agreed to submit without fighting was the trust that he reposed in his – Walter's – judgment and good faith. This was a trust that he had inherited from his father, Umqikela. At any rate, after some anxious days and nights, practically unarmed and surrounded by as many as 3 000 armed warriors in a state of tension, Stanford induced Sigcawu to sign the treaty of submission. Sigcawu did so on March 17, 1894, two days before the expiry of the period of grace, and two days before Nqwiliso and the minor chiefs of Western Pondoland signed a similar treaty with Maj Elliot.

Macquarrie's account says: "Rhodes, the prime minister, was actually in Cape Town at the time, but during the following month he visited Pondoland and met Sigcawu at Palmerton Mission, near Lusikisiki." There are conflicting accounts of this meeting, but according to Walter himself in *The Reminiscences*, "so far was Sigcawu removed from 'the frightened chief, the cowed and submissive potentate', that some accounts describe, that when he left the Palmerton meeting, he seemed to ignore the prime minister's valedictory greeting." This incident, trivial in itself, appears to have had consequences for both Sigcawu and Stanford.

> "When Sigcawu later became disloyal and troublesome, and Stanford pleaded with the prime minister for considerate and merciful treatment, Rhodes rebuked Stanford sharply for exceeding his powers as an official, and persisted in his rigorous treatment of Sigcawu. The chief had recourse to the law; was vindicated by Chief Justice Sir Henry de Villiers; and returned

SIGCAU, CHIEF OF THE PONDOS
Photographed by Gordon and Smith, Cape Town

Sigcau, Chief of the Pondos, who is about thirty years of age, has just been visiting Cape Town. He was greatly impressed with what he saw. His grandfather, Faku, was renowned as the cruellest Chief in Pondoland. Sigcau is clad in European garments, but has still much to learn. He is very superstitious, and was accompanied in his sight-seeing excursions by his witch-doctor.

Sigcau, Chief of the Pondos. Illustration for The Graphic, *13 April 1895.*
© *Look and Learn*

Sir Henry de Villiers

51

exonerated to the bosom of his tribe – as Stanford had urged. Rhodes reacted by removing Pondoland affairs from Stanford's charge.

"Despite this incident and several others, Stanford appears to have been profoundly affected by the tremendous personality, and indeed, magnanimity, of Rhodes, and tells how, near the end of his life, Rhodes offered him an apology for his treatment."

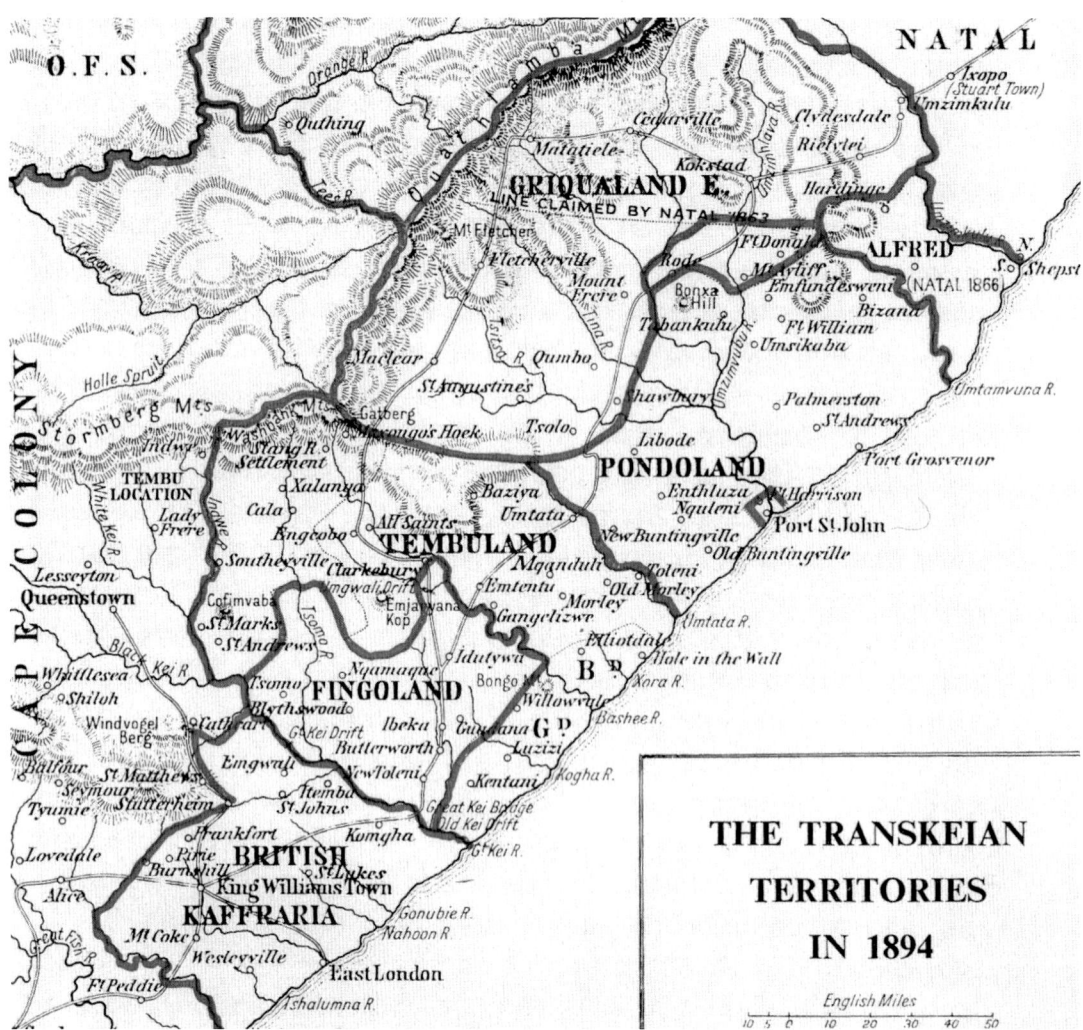

When Sir Gordon Sprigg became prime minister again in 1896, he offered Walter an appointment as Under-Secretary for Native Affairs – headship of the Native Affairs Department, with headquarters in Cape Town. However, upon arriving in the capital, Walter found that under the "Rhodes regime, the really responsible work had gone into the hands of the Secretary to the Prime Minister". He would not assume office under those conditions. The prime minister was overseas, and no one had the authority to make the necessary changes. When Sprigg returned, however, he immediately agreed to restore the department and the under-secretaryship to their proper status. Walter took up his duties at once.

It was during this period that Walter and Alice's next child was born in Cape Town – Helen Rose – on January 6, 1898.

Alice, Helen and Arthur in about 1900

A change of government followed, and in 1899 the new prime minister, W.P. Schreiner, accompanied by Walter, set off on a celebrated tour of the Eastern Province that Schreiner described as his "road to Damascus" – so profound a change did it make to his views on native policy and his attitude to natives in general.

When the South African War began (October 1899), Maj (Sir) Henry Elliot was placed in military command of the Transkeian Territories. Walter Stanford was attached to General Buller's staff, and it was arranged that in all military questions touching the Transkeian Territories, he should be the channel of communication. However, when the Boer forces invaded the Cape Colony and Natal, Walter was sent at once to the Territories, at the request of the Governor Sir Alfred Milner. There he commanded the East Griqualand Field Force, in which was incorporated the East Griqualand Mounted Rifles – the corps that he himself had founded in Kokstad. At the close of the war, he was awarded the C.B. (Military Class) and gazetted Colonel in the Cape Colonial Forces (1902).

In early 1901, it had been decided, under Walter's leadership, to establish an African township near Maitland in the Cape. This was to consist of brick houses with good facilities. However, the bubonic plague broke out in Cape Town and the civil authorities located a field hospital and an isolation camp on a site adjoining the military camp at Uitvlugt. A contact camp was established alongside it, comprising prefabricated buildings purchased from the military. Within a short time, they grew into a full community. Sometime in 1902, its name was changed to Ndabeni – the nickname given by indigenous people to Sir Walter Stanford, who was already prominent in the recognition of indigenous rights in the Cape.

Ndabeni, Cape Town's first African township, in 1905. Set up on Crown land at Uitvlug, near Maitland. In 1901, it was named, at the residents' request, after Stanford, who chaired the commission responsible. **Cape Argus Weekly, 29 March 1905.**

(In 2010, this was confirmed in the *National Library of South Africa Quarterly Bulletin 64* (3): "It was his (Sir W.S.) popularity which led to the name Ndabeni being given by the inhabitants to the first African township outside Cape Town.")

Walter Stanford, circa 1900

By 1902, Sir Henry Elliot was 85 years old, and he retired from the Chief Magistracy of Tembuland. The Government decided to consolidate the Territories under one Chief Magistrate. Walter Stanford was appointed to this new post, and as we have already seen, the next two highest offices in the Transkeian Territories were held by his brothers, Robert and Arthur.

Walter and Alice's last daughter, Eileen Mary, was born in Rondebosch in October of the same year.

From 1903–1905, Walter Stanford was a member of the South African Native Affairs Commission, which recommended that "a central native college, or similar institution, be established and aided by the various states for training native teachers in order to afford the opportunity for higher education to native students". Walter also concurred with the commission's recommendations to provide the natives with separate representation in Parliament. In a discussion with W.T. Welsh (*South African Outlook*, October 1933) he stated that in doing so, he had in mind the representation of natives by natives, which the Cape Constitution did not prohibit.

In 1904, the Prime Minister, Dr Jameson, recalled him to the headship of the Native Affairs Department in Cape Town, but asked him to retain also his office as Chief Magistrate of the Transkeian Territories. He continued to live in Cape Town until 1907, when his heart was showing such signs of strain and his throat giving so much recurring trouble that medical opinion was opposed to further official duty. At his request, the government permitted him to retire at age 57.

This allowed him a period of rest and freedom from responsibility, which in turn brought such an improvement to his health that, on Dr Jameson's suggestion, he stood for Parliament in 1908. He won the seat and was returned for Tembuland. He sat in the last Cape Parliament as an Independent, but his views were so close to those of W.P. Schreiner that he became known as Man Friday to the latter's Robinson Crusoe.

In 1908, the South African National Convention was set up to discuss the future constitution of the Union of South Africa; incorporating the four separate colonies into one country. Schreiner was nominated as a delegate, but he had already undertaken the defence of the Zulu paramount chief, Dinizulu, who was charged with sedition in connection with the rebellion of 1906.

The trial coincided with the first sittings of the Convention. Efforts to have the trial postponed were unsuccessful, and William Schreiner felt himself obliged to defend Dinizulu and to withdraw from the delegation to the convention. Merriman, probably at the suggestion of Chief Justice Sir Henry de Villiers, appointed Stanford as an Independent and an authority on native affairs.

William Philip Schreiner

It was at the Convention that Walter Stanford moved a resolution that, according to *The Reminiscences*, many South Africans today:

"recognise as the most momentous, and that posterity may yet regard as the most far-sighted, to be placed before the Convention. Stanford was a South African of the third generation; a colonial from the Border area; a native administrator with a lifetime of service behind him and a reputation for balanced judgement and prudent service to the State among the Bantu tribes. Yet, he proposed, as any Whitehall official might have done, "that all subjects of His Majesty resident in South Africa shall be entitled to franchise rights, irrespective of race or colour upon such qualifications as may be determined by this Convention.

"In proposing the motion, he referred to the Transkeian Territories General Council as virtually a Parliament. The natives, he maintained, saw the use of the franchise and took the full benefit of it. Where they had grievances, they brought these before their members. The outlet for a grievance existed, and it was not left to simmer in the minds of the natives until it led to disorder and, perhaps, rebellion. The experience of South Africa in this respect had been, he continued, the experience of New Zealand and the United States. Experience in other parts of South Africa showed that any attempt at repression was dangerous. The franchise, in effect, was the crux of the whole native question in South Africa."

Walter Stanford with John Xavier Merriman, the last Prime Minister of the Cape Colony

He also raised objections to discrimination on the grounds of colour when the topic of franchise for women was discussed, along with eligibility for election to the Parliaments.

His motion sparked a fierce debate which was only resolved after a special committee was set up to bring recommendations to the Convention. Despite his reputation and his experience of native life, he was unable to persuade the Convention to adopt a general native franchise. The Convention did, however, agree to preserve the existing Cape franchise and to entrench it in the South Africa Act.

After the Union of South Africa in 1909, both Schreiner and Walter Stanford were nominated to the new Senate. According to Sir Edgar Walton in *The Inner History of the National Convention* , this was 'on the grounds mainly of their thorough acquaintance, by reason of the official experience or otherwise, with the reasonable wants and wishes of the Coloured races in South Africa". Here, in connection with the Natives' Land Act of 1913, Walter, who had long favoured communal franchises for Bantu and Indians, declared reluctantly for territorial segregation as the only means of securing any land at all for the natives.

FIRST SESSION SOUTH AFRICAN NATIONAL CONVENTION

DURBAN, OCTOBER 1908

BACK ROW: Sir Walter Stanford. G.R. Hofmeyr. Sir George Plowman. Hon. C.J. Smyth. W.B. Morcom.

2ND ROW BACK: Sir Meiring Beck. Sir Albert Browne. G.H. Maasdorp. Hon. J.W. Jagger. Sir Thomas Hyslop.
               Sir Charles Coghlan. Sir Edgar Walton. Sir Lewis Michell. A.M.N. de Villiers.

2ND ROW FRONT: Sir Starr Jameson. General de la Rey. Sir Thomas Smartt. Hon. H.C. van Heerden. General Hertzog.
                Rt. Hon. F.S. Malan. Col. The Hon. E.H. Greene. General de Wet. General Schalk Burger. H.L. Lindsey.
                Sir George Farrar. General Smuts. Sir Percy Fitzpatrick. Sir Ernest Kilpin.

4TH ROW FRONT: Rt. Hon. J.X. Merriman. Pres. M.T. Steyn. Rt. Hon. A. Fischer. Rt. Hon. Sir Frederick Moor.
                Rt. Hon. Lord de Villiers. Rt. Hon. General Botha. Hon. J.W. Sauer. Hon. H.C. Hull. Sir William Milton.

11. Jonex, the son of Merri Man, with the chief men of the nation saileth for Dur-Ban. Some Cape delegates to the National Convention, 1908. (Left to right: J. W. Sauer, J. X. Merriman, L. S. Jameson, T. W. Smartt, W. E. M. Stanford, J. W. Jagger, Sir John H. de Villiers.) From *The Owl* of 9 October 1908.

FROM LEFT TO RIGHT, STANDING: *Alice, Arthur, Elliot, Helen. Sitting: Granny Alice, Eileen, Harry and Dorothy Ruffel, Ganku*

Meanwhile, in 1911, Walter and Alice's eldest daughter, Dorothy, married Harry Ruffel, who came from a farming family in Essex, England. This was an occasion that brought together all the family in Stellenbosch. It was their firstborn, Edmund, Walter's first grandchild who gave him the nickname 'Ganku'. Thereafter he was always known as Ganku throughout the family.

World War I separated Walter from his friend and colleague, William Schreiner, who became High Commissioner in London. Walter took up recruiting work in Cape Town and helped to found the Cape Corps as an Imperial Unit. Later, he became its Honorary Colonel. In November 1914, he was requested by the government to undertake special duty in Griqualand East. He at once consented, and left for Pretoria. There he learned details of serious unrest among the natives in the districts of Maclear, Mount Fletcher and Matatiele, and was given civil and military control in those areas in order to deal with the disturbances.

Colonel Walter Stanford on Rondebosch Common

His *Reminiscences* virtually ends with the National Convention, so we do not have his own account of this special duty. He was 64 at the time. The following account, included in Volume II of the *Reminiscences* and written by Mr A.L. Barrett, who was, at Walter's request seconded to him as his secretary, illustrates the vigour of his personality and the veneration that he inspired among the African people:

"There had been genuine unrest among the native tribes along the Basutoland border (Matatiele, Mount Fletcher, Maclear) over East Coast Fever restrictions, and it was suspected that agents wishing to increase General Botha's difficulties had been at work fomenting the trouble. Anyway, several cattle tanks have been dynamited and – recognised as an opening gambit in a native rising – a trading station had been looted and burned down. The South African Mounted Infantry, Transkei Mounted Rifles and East Griqualand Mounted Rifles had been hurriedly mobilised, motor cars being extensively used for the first time; and every available man had been despatched to Matatiele.

Walter in later years

"On our arrival we found that the Chief Magistrate (Mr W.T. Brownlee) and my old friend, Walter Carmichael, were already there, and that a great meeting of natives had been summoned by Mr Brownlee for the following morning."

"…It was attended by a great concourse of natives, many of whom were said to have short stabbing assegais concealed under their blankets, while we of the official party were sheltered, quite without our knowledge, by cross-fire from machine guns stationed behind two windows of the Magistrate's office.

"The first speaker was Chief Magistrate Mr W.T. Brownlee. He reasoned patiently and with eloquence, but the natives were in no mood for reason, and their replies were truculent. Then Stanford rose to his feet. Before he had said one word there fell a hush. It was as if a ghost had arisen to rebuke them. All the older men knew and revered him, and his presence came as a complete surprise.

"There was no more appeasement. The old warrior trounced them roundly, and none answered a word. His eyes were blazing and his voice shook with anger. He was ashamed of them. Did they know that the king was at war? Did they realise that those who troubled the king's government at such a time were running grave risks and richly deserved the punishment that would surely descend upon them? Were they mad? Did they forget that their land, the lifeblood of their tribal life, was subject to forfeiture for rebellion? Or were they lending their ears to treacherous counsel which might indeed be aimed at that very thing?

"I never saw such a complete turning of the tables, such a triumph of personality, so telling an example of his instinct for doing the right thing at the crucial moment.

"There were some halting apologies from the other side; the meeting was dismissed, and the people went sheepishly home.

"So far as I can remember, his personal report dealt mainly with detailed modification of the East Coast Fever rules with a view to reducing friction. As a former chief magistrate, he was very conscious of the ambiguous position in which his sudden advent had placed Mr Brownlee, and no doubt he intentionally minimised the part he had been called upon to play. The truth of the matter was that in Pretoria, an armed outbreak had been regarded as inevitable; it must be put down firmly, but not ruthlessly; and there was no other hand to which both aspects of that duty could so surely be entrusted.

"He had not intended to take a prominent part at the meeting. He was to come in later to take command as soon as actual fighting began; but there is no doubt in my mind that his timely intervention averted quite serious bloodshed."

Macquarrie goes on to state:

"As Mr Barrett relates, Stanford's investigation showed that there were genuine grievances in regard to dipping regulations. Agitators unsympathetic to the war effort had seized their chance to exploit these. Recommendations made by Stanford were acted upon, and he returned to the Cape and his voluntary recruiting work.

"In January 1918, the post of Director of Recruiting fell vacant. The South African Brigade had suffered heavy casualties, and there was a possibility of it losing its identity as a brigade altogether. Colonel Mentz, Minister of Defence, asked Stanford to fill the vacancy. He accepted the appointment, although it entailed moving to Pretoria, a town with an altitude liable to aggravate heart trouble (he was then 68). Happily, he was able to leave Pretoria the following year, by which time he had become Commissioner for Returned Soldiers.

Colonel Walter Stanford (photograph by courtesy of A.D.M. Walker)

"Back at the Cape, he notes in his diary: 'Dr Hugh Smith examined me this morning and advised I should not return to Pretoria. Thinks I shall pull round here… I report accordingly. It now remains for a successor to be found. I think I am entitled to a month's leave, but did not press it.'

"It was not until the end of July 1919 that he was able to hand over all official duties. His services were recognised with the K.B.E., which was gazetted at the same time as the D.S.O. awarded to his son, Arthur, for services in France in the Royal Field Artillery."

8090 THE LONDON GAZETTE, 27 JUNE, 1919.
UNION OF SOUTH AFRICA.
To be Knights Commanders of the Civil Division of the said Most Excellent Order :—
Senator Colonel the Honourable Walter Ernest,
Mortimer Stanford, C.B., C.M.G., O.B.E,
Director of war recruiting and Commissioner
for returned soldiers.

Despite being in his 70s, and at a time when one might have expected him to enjoy a more retired life, Walter continued his senate work. He remained active in other aspects, too, and in 1920 helped found the 1820 Memorial Settlers' Association, becoming chairman for the Cape area. He served as a steward of the South African Turf Club for nearly 20 years, and for a time was chairman and honorary judge on the racecourse.

The Western Province Agricultural Society, the National Society, and church work claimed some of his leisure, and when the Community Chest of Cape Town, a well-known and popular organisation, was founded, not without opposition, he undertook the chairmanship.

Throughout 1925, Alice's health gave cause for anxiety, and she spent some time in a nursing home in Cape Town. She recovered, but in her interests, Sir Walter decided to move permanently from Stellenbosch to Rondebosch, a suburb of Cape Town. They continued to enjoy family occasions, and there are a number of photographs recording these.

In 1927, the question of a flag for the Union was debated in Parliament. General Hertzog's proposal was so unpopular among South Africans of British origin that the Flag Organisation arose to fight it. Walter Stanford was Chairman of the Central Executive for the Cape Province. Branches were formed throughout the Union, and a conference took place at Bloemfontein. Fortunately, the controversy, which was rapidly becoming bitter, ended in a more or less satisfactory compromise for all parties. For the time being.

In the same year, the University of Cape Town bestowed upon him the honorary degree of Doctor of Laws – a peculiarly appropriate tribute to a man who had made and administered the law throughout most of his working life, and an honour that he greatly valued.

Neither Walter Stanford nor Dr A.W. Roberts were renominated to the Senate in 1929 (he was 79 by then). They were both old men, but in full mental and physical vigour. Between them, they had well over a century's worth of experience in native life and thought.

Stanford family group, circa 1930s, probably at Constantia
STANDING, LEFT TO RIGHT: *Alec Carswell-Smith, Dorothy, Arthur, Helen, Elliot*
SEATED, LEFT TO RIGHT: *Ganku, Eileen, Effy, Alice, Granny Alice and unknown*

In 1933, Sir Walter and Lady Stanford celebrated their golden wedding anniversary. At this, their last social function, they were surrounded by their children and grandchildren, as well as their best man, Mr Cumming, and their flowergirl, Miss Godlonton. Soon afterwards, Sir Walter became ill and died, on September 9, 1933, at the advanced aged of 83.

In his summing up of the man, Macquarrie says:

> "The most casual reading of his *Reminiscences* cannot fail to impress one with the warmth of his goodwill towards his European masters, acquaintances, colleagues, and sometimes rivals, in all grades of society, from prime ministers to the humblest of traders. The same warmth of heart is displayed towards the native population which he did so much to pacify and to bring with a minimum of force within the orbit of Western civilisation.

Sir Walter and Lady Stanford on the occasion of their golden wedding anniversary, June 1933

> "With the natives, too, rank plays but little part; he included among his friends both native chiefs like George Moshesh and Sigcawu, and lowly policemen like Thomas Poswayo. He knew these native chiefs, Dalasile, Umqikela, Sigcawu, Umhlangaso and the rest, before they came under the control of the white man, when they were indeed chiefs, ruling according to native tradition and custom. He was no blind sentimentalist, no theorist subscribing to Rousseau's belief in the 'noble savage'. No one knew better than Stanford the prevalence among tribal Africans of customs and practices repugnant to the civilised mind and heart. His memoirs, however, illustrate to a remarkable degree the admirable human qualities, indeed civilised qualities, possessed by these people – their chivalry in war towards women and children; their faith in and loyalty towards Europeans whom they trusted, their sagacity and eloquence in debate, their restraint under provocation, and their fortitude and dignity in adversity. The sentiments expressed in the *Reminiscences* are a tribute to the men he worked with and warred against and, in particular, to the mental and moral stature of the African people whom he knew so well. These sentiments are no less worthy a tribute to the man who held them, to Stanford himself."

When he died, General Smuts wrote to his widow:

> "Sir Walter Stanford I had counted for many years among those of my friends on whom I could rely most implicitly for wise counsel and loyal support. To me, too, it is a deep sorrow that he has passed away. Our consolation is that he has had an exceptional record of great service to his country, and that he leaves behind a record of which we are all very proud."

St. Paul's Church Record in October 1933 said this of him:

"A great man has gone from us. Sir Walter Stanford was great in his fine sense of justice, his insight, his wisdom; great in his loyalty and sincerity, greater still in his wonderful lowliness of heart. We were honoured in having him as a member of our Church Council, and could always rely upon him to give the soundest advice, and once he had spoken there was no need for more to be said. He brought conviction, for he had such clear understanding and found the way to the heart of a perplexing difficulty, not hastily, not hesitatingly, but with quiet certainty and modesty.

"His was a long life but a very full life, and a life of fruitful service. We were very privileged to have him in our midst. He has passed to the realm of larger opportunity, but he leaves us conscious of a great nobility of character, of worthy achievements, of splendid example. His works do follow him and the love that they wrought!"

The *Kokstad Advertiser* of September 22, 1933, wrote:

"And perhaps the greatest of them all was Sir Walter Stanford. As is always the case, his success was achieved not by intellect or suppleness, but by character. The natives learned that they could trust him, and he never betrayed their trust. It was men of his type and generation whose character created settled government throughout wide areas of Africa and the East. It is sometimes claimed that the breed has become extinct – that young men now coming forward have a lower sense of responsibility and a higher measure of self-seeking in their composition. But we do not believe it. But if the danger does grow acute, the example of Sir Walter Stanford will be useful for many a day as a check and an inspiration to those who succeed him. The Transkeian Territories, to-day plunged in gloom by the loss of their father, may well say: 'If you ask his monument, look around.'"

Ganku with his grandson, Gavin Relly, circa 1928

Although there were many formal tributes paid to him throughout his life and after his death by many senior and famous people, he was always given great affection by his children and grandchildren who saw him as a very human man. He always had dogs, and in the last years of his life regularly walked them in Rondebosch on what is now called Stanford Road after him.

His eldest granddaughter, Lois (my mother), said of him: "My grandfather was a tall man, about 6ft 2in, a very good horseman who carried himself with distinction. Within the family, he was gentle, never raised his voice in anger and was beloved by his children and grandchildren. He must, however, have had the determination and sternness of character needed to become the successful man he was."

Another of his granddaughters, Allison, remembered him doing his exercises every morning. She and her sister Dorothy used to hide under his kneehole desk to watch him doing them in his long johns. She thinks he must have known they were there, but never let on!

His grandson, Bruce Relly, remembers being allowed, as a treat, to watch him shaving. Clearly he was a man who did not stand on his dignity with his grandchildren.

He was always kind and modest. Whenever he achieved anything, he always said it was really someone else who should take the credit. Amongst the many letters of condolence Alice, his widow, and the family received after his death, the words used to describe him included: "courteous"; "courageous"; "liberal"; and "thoughtful". However, the one that appeared most often on the personal notes was "lovable".

Lois also tells a delightful story that illustrates much of Ganku's character and standing:

"Towards the end of the 19th century, my grandfather was Chief Magistrate in the Transkei, a huge territory on the east coast of South Africa. He was much beloved by the native tribes there, and since he had grown up in that part of the world, he spoke their language – Xhosa – as well as he spoke English.

"I have lately come across a description of him in a book written in 1895 and I quote from it:

'The Chief Magistrate's native name was Ndabeni, which means the one of counsel. He was a man of vast experience in respect of the natives, and moreover he did not belong to that highly moral, but sometimes inconvenient class of officials who are known as the hide-bound; that is to say his ideas ranged beyond the length of the longest piece of red-tape in his office, and he knew for a certainty that things existed which could not be wrapped up in foolscap paper. He was one moreover, who trusted much to his own considerable personal influence, and he believed in using the talents of such of his subordinates as possessed faculties similar to his own in this respect.'

"A little later in the same account, a native chief is quoted as saying: 'Ndabeni is a great man, he has eyes all round his head. His words are good to hear.'

"One day, a black sergeant of police came to Ganku and said: 'Ndabeni, my wife has had a son and I would like to give him to you to be your son.' Ganku responded with all due solemnity, but said that the baby would need to be brought up by his own mother. The child was called Pinkerton, for reasons I have never been able to fathom.

"Shortly after this, Ganku left the Transkei and was based in Cape Town, where he had an illustrious career. But when Pinkerton was 16, he decided he would go to the Cape and seek his white father. He set off walking the few hundred miles from the Transkei. Along the way, he stayed in 'locations', or native quarters outside European towns. When he told people he was going to find Ndabeni, they would feed and lodge him and wave him on.

"At last he arrived at Ganku's house and said: 'Ndabeni, here I am.' Thereafter, Ganku housed him and apprenticed him to a local garage. After seven years he became Ganku's chauffeur.

"When I stayed with Granny and Ganku, it was Pinkerton who drove me around and, indeed it was he who really taught me to drive. He was a very good-looking man and always very smartly dressed in his chauffeur's uniform and gauntlet gloves. I said to him once: 'The girls like you, don't they Pinkerton?' and he said: 'Oh Miss Loeess, it is because I am so pretty!'

"Ganku died in 1933 and Granny moved out to Somerset West. I went on to different scenes and adventures. But in 1947, I took Malcolm and Frances out to South Africa to meet their grandparents there. One day, I was walking down Adderley Street, the main broad street of Cape Town, when I heard a voice crying: 'Miss Loeess, Miss Loeess!' Turning, I saw Pinkerton running down towards me. Smartly dressed as ever, he was now in the uniform of Commissionaire to one of the big shops. And so we stood and beamed at each other while the pedestrian traffic eddied around us."

Sir Walter Stanford's obituary was published in the *Cape Argus*:

LOSS TO SENATE AND ASSEMBLY
DEATH OF SIR WALTER STANFORD

Life of service in cause of natives

The *Argus* regrets to announce the death of Sir Walter Stanford, one of the Senators appointed at the time of Union for his experience and knowledge of the "reasonable wants and wishes of the coloured races."

Walter Ernest Mortimer Stanford, who died at his home, Lindani, Rondebosch, early this morning, was born at Alice, Cape Colony, in 1850. His father, Captain William Stanford, commanded a native contingent in the Kaffir War of 1850, and died when Walter was only six years of age.

Being in a critical state of health, he was sent to the native territories and remained there for four years. He later went to Lovedale College to be educated and in these surroundings imbibed an intelligent and intimate knowledge of the native peoples.

When 50 years later he pleaded at the National Convention for the fullest native franchise he was justifiably able to say that his whole life's work had been a study of the Bantu people.

That work he began when he was but 14 years of age. He was placed in the public service as a clerk to the Tambookie agent at Glen Grey, and next in Tembuland. Eight years later he was promoted as clerk to the magistrate at Queenstown, and obtained his first magistracy in 1876 with Dalasile's people.

The last Xhosa war

The clouds portending a renewal of serious trouble began to appear. Two years after the storm broke and the ninth and last Xhosa War was fought to a finish.

At the time Mr Stanford was 28 years of age, and with other magistrates in the Transkei he had often to exchange the pen for the sword in leading Colonial emergency troops.

The issues of that period were and still seem confused to the reader of today, but primarily their interpretation must be sought in the recurring clash of advancing white civilisation and a stubborn native patriotism.

It would be difficult to overrate the tasks and trials which beset the Transkeian magistrates during this upheaval. Not only had the Colonial Parliament to be guided as well as obeyed, but High Commissioner and Cape Cabinet were often at variance.

While political reputations fell fast and thick it is abundant testimony to the sound training of the Kaffrarian judiciary that theirs remained unchallengeable. Several lost their lives in their duty; others lived to reconstruct native government on a sounder and more equitable footing.

Chief Magistrate

Mr Stanford's qualifications brought him to the fore, and in 1885 he was appointed Chief Magistrate of Griqualand East. In that capacity and also that of Superintendent of Native Affairs and Secretary of the Native Department, he conducted in statesmanlike manner a number of important treaties and settlements with Kaffir clans, particularly the annexation of Pondoland to the Cape Colony. The whole of these negotiations were handled, and successfully concluded by him.

At the commencement of the South African War, with the rank of Lieut-Colonel, he commanded the forces in East Griqualand. He also served under Major Elliot and was mentioned in dispatches.

Retiring, on the urgent advice of his doctor, from the Government service before Union, he became member in the Cape Assembly for Tembuland, and in that capacity was appointed a member of the National Convention of 1909. His unique knowledge of, and sympathy with, the native rendered his work on the Commission invaluable.

Colonel Stanford's part in that great conference is plainly manifested in Sir Edgar Walton's book, "The Inner Story of the National Convention".

The Franchise

True to his own unerring knowledge of the Transkeian native, he moved that they should be entitled to the franchise. He laid stress on the extraordinary extent to which natives had, in the last 30 years, put aside their tribal past and availed themselves of the methods of civilisation, emphasising the admirable way they were conducting their Native Council and had raised their own taxes.

In few things, however, was the Convention on more thorny ground than the enfranchisement of the native. The question was inevitably shelved, to be decided by the Union Parliament thereafter.

Sir Walter received his C.B. in 1901 and C.M.G. the following year. In 1919 he was created K.B.E. At Union he was made a Senator by reason of his experience and knowledge of the coloured and native races.

In that capacity he faithfully watched the interest of the natives during his service in the Upper House.

In June of this year Col. Sir Walter and Lady Stanford relived the scenes of their original wedding day, celebrated on June 7, 1883, at Port Elizabeth – 50 years ago.

His Paramount Concern

"To-day I have 18 grandchildren to keep me young" said Sir Walter on the occasion in an interview with a representative of The Argus. "They are my chief pleasure, with my books and dogs. But I still keep up with several interests with which I have been closely identified all my life.

"My two brothers and I were noted as horsemen and drove the four-in-hand for a number of years: I follow the horses now – but at the races, and am vice-president of the South African Turf Club.

"Being a descendant on both sides of the family of the 1820 Settlers, the present association engages my interests and I serve on the committee as well as on that of the National Society.

"The natives of South Africa remain the paramount concern in my life and I still follow their affairs closely. I am very happy at the way the younger generation has handled its heritage in this country. They have well maintained what they had to maintain.

"This was an almost autocratic position in relation to the native people of the county who respond, I have found, to just treatment and are capable of wonderful loyalty and self-sacrifice. Young South Africa is handling that trust well."

CHAPTER VI

Sarah Alice Stanford, née Walker

Alice, as she was always called, was born in King Williams Town in January 1859, the third child of 11 born to Joseph and Dorothy Walker. Sadly, Ellen Margaret, their second child, died before Alice was born. The family was a close and loving one, and was relatively prosperous, as Joseph was a successful merchant in Port Elizabeth. She met and fell in love with Walter Ernest Mortimer Stanford, and their marriage was set for June 1883. It must have been disappointing for her that her father was in England and unable to attend her wedding.

He wrote to her in April 1883 thus:

7 Gloucester Road,
Finsbury Park N.,
April 4 1883

My dear Alice,

Thank you very much for your kind note. Thinking I was going off to Glasgow yesterday, I got all my letters to your dear Mother forward on Monday evening, so I am a little at liberty to give you a report to share. It quite depends upon our desires and occupation how time passes. I suppose you would get the information

Sarah Alice Walker, before her marriage

of the Gaiths' arrival three days after you wrote, but you would not hear from me till just about a month after you wrote on the March 10, and then you were looking for news!

I am so sorry this trip of mine came when it did for you both — because if you had left us for all practical

66

purposes for the time being I might as well have been in England as the Cape Colony as far as you were concerned. It makes me very sad to think I am going to lose you tho I lose you under circumstance which could not to my thinking be more favourable. You have always been a dear little gentle daughter to me – very dear to me as you always will be. I have told your dear Mother to do all that is necessary for I shall not be out in time to do anything – it's not right but bless you I can't help it. I feel as if I was in a sort of vice. I am glad Walter does not object – he is a reasonable fellow and knows something of the worry I have endured. When I saw what those Squatters were up to I knew Cumming could not get away as soon as he thought for. I hope matters will go on comfortably.

I am very glad you are going in for bathing – it will do you good. I always think of a piece of advice which Dr. Fitzgerald once gave me about bathing – never go to bathe without having some woollen thing to stand on while you are drying yourself and dressing. I have never neglected this piece of advice and let me empress it upon you, an old coat or a petticoat will answer.

You will see by my letters that I have been a good deal at Levys – they are awfully kind to me. Abby & Julia also, they are nice girls, but pleasure is all they think about. The father and mother are a little disgusted I think with it, but very proud of them notwithstanding. Abby is really accomplished – she sings & plays splendidly, and I saw some painting of hers on china, which astonished me. She is very tall and both are very stylish & dress in the extreme of fashion. Julia is short & much thinner. She is the idol of her husband, who is well off and being a Lady, a gentleman tailor can indulge her in any extravagance of dress and otherwise.

You will see by my letters that I was driving in Hyde Park yesterday looking at all the rank & fashion of Vanity Fair – it was a glorious afternoon, but all the time I kept thinking of you all working up in the nursery as if your living depended upon it – pleasant reflections in Rotten Row! It is very nice to hear you are all well and truly thankful I am for that blessing as well that I myself enjoy such good health. When you write to Walter give him my love and tell him anything about me that you think will interest him. I do not know of anyone who I could welcome with more cordiality into the family & treat with more confidence.

Best love from your affectionate Father
JW

Tell Arthur I value his letters and as I have not written to him, I have bought him an interesting book "Diary of a bad boy"

Arthur, Alice's brother, would have been 15 years old at the time of this letter. Despite her father's absence, she and Walter were married in June in Port Elizabeth, and moved immediately to live in Engcobo in the Transkei. She must, over the years, have had some difficult and anxious times, worrying about her husband's safety and health. She remained loyally supportive throughout his career. She received from her father, Joseph, another letter in October 1907, about the time that Walter stood for Parliament. It demonstrated the intimacy of her family relationships:

P.E. 4 Oct 1907

My dear Alice,

You wrote to me on Monday & I wrote to you on Tuesday. After not writing to each other for such a long time, it shows there must have been some mysterious influence at work to impel us to take up our pens almost at the same time. I suppose we must ascribe it to the telepathic communication which passes unconsciously between our minds and set our pens in motion. I made up my mind when I got your nice interesting letter last evening as we were sitting round the table that I would answer it at once & so try and keep the ball rolling. I often feel I want to hear from you & then almost directly a letter comes from you, showing we have been thinking about each other. The subject of your letter which struck me most was the cuteness & confidence of your little Eileen (Walter and Alice's youngest daughter) in supplying herself with sweets. The cleverness of children often surprises me. We have many specimens of it with our two pickles – Charlie (one of Joseph's grandsons by his daughter, Etheline May, who was always called 'May') especially is very quick at repartée & in finding excuses for his misdoings, which are not few. But I don't know anything more clever than your little chap's 'use' of her credit with her grocer.

It would have been a pity to have lost the distinguished honour of meeting the Maynards. It's almost a pity you did not discover your identity to them. To our surprise one day, Mrs M's card was brought in for your Mother, who was the only one who saw her. Your Mother was astonished to see her invalid friend turned into a healthy active woman. She says her doctor told her she would never be well, so she threw aside medicine & ever since, she had been getting better. It only proves what we all thought, that her ailments were imaginary & not real. It must be a tremendous relief to "be shot" of all those bushels of medicine bottles they carried about with them. They have been here several times, but this is the first time she has called since they stopped with us more than thirty years ago!

I see Walter & his friends have had their meeting at KWT (King WilliamsTown) & that Mr Saner did them the honour of being present. His presence you may depend was to act as a counterpoise to Walter's influence with the natives. Mr Jabavu has been getting off the track, on account of the liquour question, & I expect Saner has been sent up to put him in line with the Bund again. Yes! This sudden appeal to the country has upset any calculations. I was hoping Walter would have a year's rest before embarking on politics. I suppose Walter will have the whole of the trader influence against him. These people won't forgive him for thwarting their land grabbing. However, his return will be a matter of organization, & if he is well supported in this, there can be no fear of his return. I hope he won't overdo it in speaking too much, tho he is bound to do a certain amount.

Sarah Alice Stanford (née Walker)

I don't seem to have anything to tell you. We have Auntie with us & Dorothy Cleverly. (Dorothy cleverly married Joseph's youngest son, Harold, the following year. She was sometimes referred to as Dory.) Auntie talks of going tomorrow. We laugh at her and want to know why she should hurry, but she seems to think she has been long enough away from poor old Aunt Jinny. Her cold is better, but it has pulled her down & she does not look as well as when she first arrived. She seems to have a good time at E. London. The two little Fish boys seem very fond of her & they are paragons of good behaviour & I am afraid our two mischievous & manly rapscallions must compare with them very unfavourably. I think our boys are just what boys ought to be – they are hard to put up with some times, but they are as natural as birds. I think when I last wrote, May was labouring under one of her painful neuralgia attacks, but she is all right now & very lively. We heard from Harold since his arrival at Narrow Poort that he is better pleased with the place than he expected, but I don't think he will be at home much. He says he will have to spend next week at Cradock, doing work on the line. Dory is hoping she may see him some times. Perhaps she may, for N. Poort is only an hour & a quarter from Hanover Road, but from there to Hanover is a cart journey of two hours & trains don't run to suit weekends, but for this one would think he might spend every weekend with her. She does feel it so being cut off from all her friends. It's a long time since we heard from Kokstad.

Norwood (Joseph's second youngest child, John Norwood Walker) wrote last, but that was as far back as Sept 10. It isn't generally so long as that, so I suppose we shall hear shortly. I suppose you know Miss Baker is leaving Katie (married to Joseph's son, Arthur) – the latter thinks she can do without her. Between ourselves, your Mother is rather put out, for she says it only means that more will fall on Arthur, and a man who works as hard as he does ought to be excused from domestic cares altogether, if possible. I think so, too, but of course we don't say anything. I think Norwood & his family live a very happy ideal life. The three are devoted to each other & he has no time for anything but developing his kindly disposition, which is such a prominent feature in his character.

Since I finished the last sentence, the important subject of dinner (lunch, I suppose you would call it) has been disposed of, but it has not brought up any matter worth relating except Ben (Joseph Benjamin Mortimer Walker – Joseph's eldest son) christening Joe (May's older son) 'Joseph Gumpert' because he will not sit straight at the table. Joe was highly tickled at the idea, but protested nevertheless. Auntie has had a letter from Maud Haynes. She is taking care of Grace at Berlin. She says the latter is better for the change. Poor girl has had a long illness.

The rain has been threatening for some days & now it is coming down in earnest. It is to be hoped Walter won't be interrupted by it in his travels.

I think I may report that we are all well, except your dear old Mother, she is very lame & I am sorry to say that irritating eczema is teasing her very much. One day the latter seems to have gone & then it comes back worse than ever. Now she has just come in with another trouble – she wants me to say what she is to order from the butcher for Sunday! "for she cannot go on ordering forever "Lamb – roast beef". That's our least trouble but I suppose it's over for she has written it down & gone off with it. Kind love from your affectionate father and Mother,

JW.

Your Mother says kind love to Alice (their 4th child and second daughter) *and the children & not to forget to send her love to Elliot* (Alice's eldest son, Walter Elliot) *whenever you write. Rain coming down like fun.*

Sarah Alice Stanford in 1910

Lois wrote about her thus:

"My grandmother married Ganku when she was quite young and went with him to live in wild native territories in South Africa, often with almost no other white women around. She had grown up in Port Elizabeth, the daughter of a prosperous merchant, and had high standards in everything, from which she never deviated. She was a short woman and walked very fast, with small steps, so that she always seemed to be bustling. She could be critical and intolerant, but had a piercing sense of humour and witty tongue.

69

She loved animals and small children, but found it hard to be demonstrative towards older people. When I stayed with my grandparents, and Granny was over 70, she used to walk round the garden every day after breakfast, and her two cats would always accompany her. A charming little procession.

"She was very particular about her clothes, and when she was young, every season she ordered two outfits from her dressmaker in Port Elizabeth, so that she always had something fashionable to wear, even in the Transkei. All her daughters grew up with a sense of style and an ability to make or alter clothes skillfully.

"Granny was unable to breastfeed her babies, of whom she had seven, and brought them up on condensed milk. All of them lived long lives (except Robert, the third son). The eldest, my Uncle Eliot, lived to be 104. I have often marveled at how my grandmother achieved this, and felt much sympathy with her, since I, too, had difficulty breast-feeding and felt myself to have failed a very important exam!" (*I too, inherited this failing. Celia*)

Her other grandchildren said that Alice held deep affections and a great love for all little children and animals, especially cats. She had many homes throughout her married life, and wherever she lived, she created gardens. After Ganku died, she lived at Waterkloof in Somerset West, the home of her daughter, Helen, and her husband, Cullis Hamilton Relly, with their two boys, Gavin and Bruce. By that time, she was quite elderly. Bruce remembers her as a little reserved, and quite strict.

She died at Somerset West on December 11, 1937.

'Granny Alice with her beloved cats at Waterkloof, the home of her daughter, Helen, and her husband, Hamilton Relly

Alice, Lady Stanford, at Waterkloof in the 1930s

DESCENDANTS OF WALTER ERNEST MORTIMER STANFORD

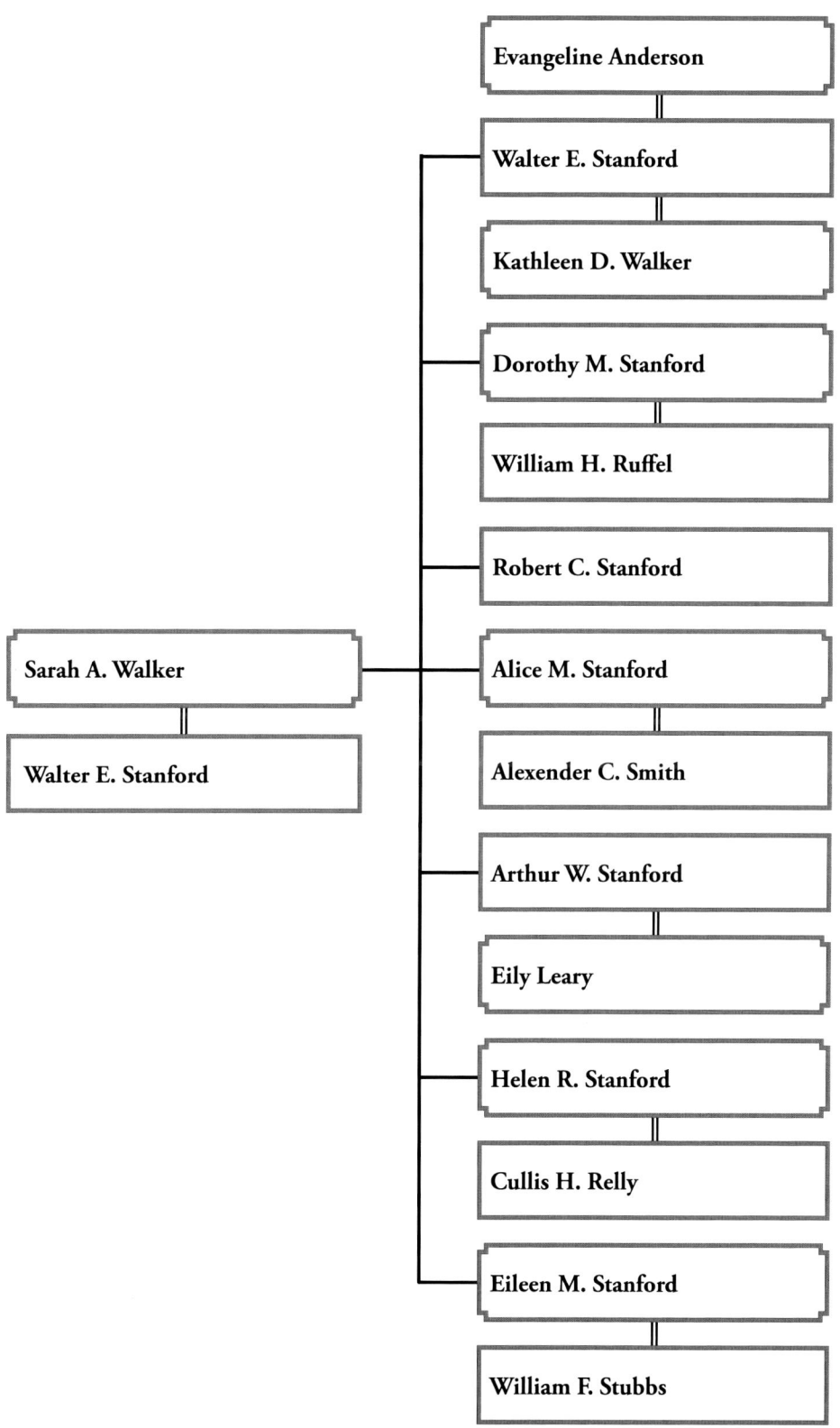

CHAPTER VII

The Third Generation Born in South Africa

Sir Walter and Lady Stanford's children – Walter Elliot Stanford

Granny Alice Stanford with Walter Elliot, aged six months

The eldest of their children was **Walter Elliot**, born in Umtata on Christmas Day 1884. He was named after Walter's friend and colleague, Sir Henry Elliot, who was Chief Magistrate to the Transkei from 1891 to 1902. Since Walter was at the time officially occupied in Encgobo, Alice had been sent to Umtata in the care of a "native constable" by Cape cart for the birth. He was always known simply as Elliot, to distinguish him from his father. Both names – Elliot and Stanford – became popular in the Transkei. Elliot recalled being held up by an ox wagon on a Transkei road where a delay in giving way irritated him. He demanded the driver's name. The reply surprised him: "Elliot Stanford!"

In 1896, when Walter was appointed Secretary of Native Affairs, the family moved to Cape Town, where Elliot attended SACS (South Africa College High School – the oldest founded public school in South Africa). Strong and athletic, he captained his school's rugby team and gained shelves full of athletic trophies.

After matriculating, he went on to the College (the forerunner of the University of Cape Town), where he continued a busy sporting and social life. He particularly enjoyed ballroom dancing! He then became one of the first Rhodes Scholars to study law at New College, Oxford, where he continued to excel at sport. Despite a very tight budget, he reveled in skiing in Switzerland. Elliot was called to the Bar at the Inns of Court. He practised law for a time in Cape Town, but at the age of 27, he decided to turn his hand to farming. He and his brother, Arthur, took over Inungi, their father's farm in East Griqualand (now KwaZulu-Natal), near Kokstad. Cynthia (Payne), Elliot's daughter, said of her father's change of career in 1911:

"For my parents, the early days on the farm must have been very lonely. My father had given up his social and business associations when he decided to desert the law and start farming with his brother on their father's farms in East Griqualand. I think he had always hankered after the freedom and openness he had known in his youth, when he had travelled about by wagon, cart or on horseback with his father, who was a magistrate in Ngcobo, Kokstad, and then Chief Magistrate of all the Transkeian Territories.

"My father had obtained a B.A. in Science at the South African College, and from there won a Rhodes scholarship to Oxford. He was called to the Bar in London and became a member of the Inner Temple. He then returned to Cape Town. He told us there came a morning when he had donned his official garb and was tying his tie, when he thought he could not spend the rest of his life in what seemed like a trap. And that was the end of his life as a barrister.

"From very small beginnings, he and Arthur built up their numbers of cattle and sheep. The old Griqua-built house, with its four small rooms, wide stoep, yellowwood floors, and lean-to kitchen at the back, expanded over the years to accommodate a growing family. It was this house that was finally, and sadly for us all, burned to the ground in a devastating veld fire in 1977."

The farm was situated alongside the great Umzimvubu River ('Home of the Hippopotamus') and had a wonderful view of Mount Currie. Ganku had bought the farm, which included three farmsteads – Inungi, Alewynspoort and Engelo – in about 1890. The Ninge range runs northwards from the Ntsizwa Mountains. The Umzimvubu River flows along the east side of the range and then plunges through it before it reaches the Ntsizwa and flows on down towards Mount Frere on its way to Port St John's. To the west of the Ninge range is the Mvenyani River, which joins the Umzimvubu River just after it emerges from the gorge and forms the boundary of Mount Frere district and Bacaland. The farm stretched from beyond the Umzimvubu, over the Ninge, to the Mvenyani. It was an area of the most wonderful varied animal habitats. To the east of the river was a small pan, where a great number of birds used to gather.

In 1914, Elliot met Evangeline Anderson while on a visit to Cape Town. Effie, as she was always known. was a member of the huge Molteno Anderson clan. Her grandfather was Sir John Molteno, the first Prime Minister of the Cape, who had 16 children. Most of her 72 first cousins lived in the Cape, and life was lived in a crowd of contemporaries. She was sent to school at St Leonards in St Andrews, Scotland. During her fourth year there, she was summoned home, as her mother, Maria (née Molteno) was dying. After her mother's death, she remained with her father as his companion and housekeeper. They travelled widely on the European continent and spent long periods in Italy. She also spent a year at a finishing school in Dresden, where she became fluent in German.

Elliot and Effie married in Cape Town in December 1914, shortly after the outbreak of World War I. When they arrived in Franklin (East Griqualand) after their honeymoon, they found that Elliot's brother, Arthur, had not come to meet them and they had to take the postcart to Kokstad. Arthur had, in fact, taken the horses and gone to enlist. As Inungi was a 'border farm', Elliot could not leave it for the duration of the war. The farmhouse lay to the west of the river and on the eastern side of the Ninge, so the river had to be forded whenever the family went to town or to visit neighbours.

By now, the house had been improved, and a large living room added where the lean-to kitchen had originally been. Despite suffering severely from asthma in the summer, Effie set to at once making a garden, and to Ganku's horror, cut down a number of trees that were obstructing the wonderful view from the house. But her efforts to settle into the house were defeated by the fact that it was a very wet summer that year, and all her new furniture and possessions, which had been sent up from Cape Town, stood on the wagon, covered by the wagon sail, on the far side of the flooded river.

It was weeks before the water subsided sufficiently for the wagon to cross, and by that time considerable damage had been done to the furniture, which had got wet and the wood had swollen. Added to which, the rats had eaten the 'riempie' (leather thongs for the seat and back) of the stinkwood dining room chairs! Effie was not a person to sit down and bemoan her misfortunes. The chair seats were repaired in the evenings and she soon had the house looking lovely.

Inungi remained a family home, much enjoyed by the wider family, and it proved to be an exciting place for Elliot and Effie's children to grow up. They enjoyed great freedom in their wild and natural environment; riding their horses and visiting people in the pony trap or on the postcart. The river played an important role in their lives, particularly affecting them when it flooded. All visitors and goods had to cross it. The mountain and forests provided wonderful habitats for birds and animals, and as the family grew, it benefited from exploring and enjoying all they had to offer.

Elliot and Effie had six children between 1916 and 1931: Sheila; Cynthia; Margaret; Eleanor; John and Philip. Cynthia vividly remembers her childhood at Inungi and describes the important role a number of their servants played in their family life.

Elliot and Effie in 1935

The 1930s, especially the early years, were times of hardship. The economic collapse plus terrible drought made produce hard to sell, and farms became almost worthless. Many farmers failed. Elliot barely survived. Economy was the order of the day and the children grew up counting pennies.

Social life at Inungi was limited by bad roads, long distances and the Umzimvubu River, which in summer cut off the farm from the neighbours and the town. The family car (he bought his first car – a 1920 Oldsmobile – in 1927) would be left on the far bank, and all access was by rowing boat, or a cable car pulled by hand on a very ragged wire. Such social life as there was consisted mainly of tennis or picnics on horseback at the river, or in the beautiful forest on the mountain. There was also a monthly church service on the Rennie's farm, with lunch and tennis. Some would ride the 20 km on horses. In the winter, there was polo.

Farming at Inungi was primitive. A few cows were milked. There was a poor market for beef, so Elliot specialised in rearing and training trek oxen (draught oxen), which found a ready market. The farm relied entirely on ox power, and the three spans of red oxen with wide horns pulling three ploughs were a special sight. Sheep farming was limited by stock theft and predation by jackals, lynx and stray dogs from the neighbouring Transkei.

Effie died in August 1952 aged 66, leaving Elliot bereft and lonely. However, two years later, he married again, this time to Kathleen Dorothy Walker, who had previously been married to F.J. Scheepers (who had died in 1951) with whom she had two children, Lynette and Michael. Kathleen was the daughter of Arthur Edward Mortimer Walker, Granny Alice (Sarah Alice Stanford)'s brother. Elliot and Kathleen were therefore first cousins, but, since Elliot was approaching 70 and Kathleen was 54 at the time of their marriage, there were no constraints on the marriage! Kathleen died in 1971, aged 71, 18 years before Elliot.

In 1964 Elliot handed over the farming responsibility to his son, John (whom I have quoted extensively in this chapter), but continued to take a keen and constructive interest as the farm began to develop along more modern lines. Sadly, in 1977 a veld fire caused the old house at Inungi to burn down, along with many prized possessions. He had lived in it for 64 years. A new, smaller house was built and he could again entertain his friends for bridge.

Elliot, like his father and grandfather, was a very fine horseman, and he continued to ride well into his 80s. His other interests were varied, and included playing bridge, cabinetmaking with lovely yellowwood and stinkwood, and breeding and schooling polo ponies. *(I still own two pieces of his yellowwood furniture, passed to me by his sister, Dorothy, my grandmother.)* He continued to play tennis and golf into his 90s, and received a new tennis racquet for his 90th birthday! He was also a talented artist whose pen and ink sketches of childhood and of life at Inungi show wit and an economy of line that is very touching. He was exceptionally well-read and actively followed politics, rugby and scientific developments. He was more interested in learning about the present than in going over the past and was known for his sharp wit. At his 100th birthday party, he made a speech without notes for more than 15 minutes. He was a remarkable man.

Two of Uncle Elliot's little sketches

In 1984, Inungi was sold after Yenzella – part of the farmland – was appropriated and joined to the Transkei. A new start was made at Rheenendal, near Knysna, where he adapted happily at the age of 100. He played bridge, drove his car, fished in the dam (and fell in!) and occasionally rode a horse.

Sydney Duval wrote an article in 'UmAfrika' marking the occasion of Elliot's 100th birthday, which fell on Christmas Day 1984:

Elliot Stanford

"A grand old man who is a living link with the Cape's distant pioneering days turned 100 on Christmas Day.

"While the centenarian was being honoured at a celebration at the Constantia home of grandson Brian Kilpin, East Griqualand was also paying tribute to one of its 'most revered sons', in Elliot Stanford, who now lives in Knysna.

"Elliot's father, Sir Walter Stanford, Chief Magistrate of Kokstad, was later instrumental in Pondoland's annexation. Elliot was born in Umtata and grew up in Kokstad at a time when control of East Griqualand had only recently come into the hands of the Cape Government. He recalls being present with his father at the massing of Pondo Impis to settle a rivalry over the chieftaincy. He was struck by the way small numbers of white officials were able to move about unmolested and to assert their authority amid all the turmoil.

"He went to school in Kokstad, then matriculated from SACS. The Old Boys' Union also honoured him at a tea party attended by Rupert de Smidt, 101, who was a year ahead of him and is the school's oldest living old boy.

"Elliot won a Rhodes scholarship to Oxford, was called to the bar in London, practised law for a time in Cape Town, and then returned to farm in East Griqualand. Farming life and the bracing climate there agreed with him, nurturing him for a ripe old age in that lovely enclave of modest prosperity, the vigorous outdoor life, horses and old-world hospitality surrounded by Transkei, Lesotho and Natal. It was there that Adam Kok and his followers found their promised land after trekking from the Free State.

"Elliot lived there for the remainder of his life, until he retired to Knysna a year ago, where he keeps busy playing bridge, or sketching pen and ink scenes from his childhood. He remembers driving a six-in-hand post cart, taking ponies over the sod walls enclosing town properties – just for the fun of it – playing polo, gymkhanas and horseracing with the Cape Mounted Rifles.

"Elliot told his hometown newspaper, *The Kokstad Advertiser*, that he deplored the breaking down of tribal authority. Blacks had been subjected to an alien system of legal discipline, eroding the authority of the chiefs and leading to discontent and tension all round.

"Well, who knows what might have happened if they had tried some other approach? No politicians on TV every night – no TV at all for that matter, no electricity, no computers and no discussions about ominous 666 signs from Revelations. Where can you drive a six-in-hand post cart in peace and quiet these days?

"All in all, Elliot's long life sounds like a very good life to remember and cherish."

Four years later, a small article appeared in *The Times* in London:

"Some years ago there was considerable correspondence in *The Times* about longevity in the legal professions. I have not examined the records of the Inns of Court, but I know that the senior member of the Inner

Temple is Walter Stanford, of Knysna, Cape Province, South Africa. He celebrated his 104th birthday last Christmas, an occasion not overlooked by his Inn. After his call to the Bar, Stanford returned to what was the Cape Colony to practise in Cape Town. However, he retired from the Bar in 1911 (yes, 1911). Those barristers with some years ahead of them will be sorry to learn that Stanford attributes his continuing good health to that wise decision. He gave up playing polo only 20 years ago and golf 10 years ago. He still enjoys a weekly game of bridge and expresses strong and incisive views on those people who have governed his country for the past 40 years."

Elliot died suddenly in December 1989, just short of his 105th birthday.

The house on the Inungi farm, built by Elliot's son, John, when he married Jo in 1954

Dorothy Maud Stanford

Ganku and Granny Alice's second child, Dorothy, was my grandmother. She was much loved, and very much respected by all her grandchildren (of which she had 11 and 19 great-grandchildren). She was born in Kokstad in 1886 and was sent to boarding school in Folkestone, Kent, probably when she was about 14. The school was Rochester House School for Young Ladies, and at the time of her schooling, it was probably run by the Misses Harsant. A few years later, it was taken over by Brampton Down School, which moved there from London.

Ganku accompanied her to England, and en route they called in at Lisbon. Upon going ashore, Ganku was asked for his passport, to which he replied "Passport? PASSPORT? I'm an English gentleman!" and walked through!

ROCHESTER HOUSE, EARL'S AVE FOLKESTONE

Where D.M.R. was at school

Dorothy Maud, aged about three years

Dorothy Maud, aged about 18

Before returning to South Africa when she finished school, she went on a tour of the more usual European capital cities. According to Veronique, Dorothy's youngest granddaughter, she had a guide book that defined the French as "a gay and happy people, fond of dancing and light wines"! She teased her French son-in-law frequently with this definition, much to his chagrin.

Another anecdote from that chapter of her life came to light when Hermione (her younger daughter and Veronique's mother) sent her a postcard announcing that she and her family (Veronique had not been born at that point) had at last reached Paris in 1948. The postcard depicted the Arc de Triomphe. Dorothy responded by asking what they had done to the Arc, as it seemed very different from how she remembered it. There followed an exchange of letters between them in which Hermione denied any change, and Dorothy insisted that something had changed. Some months later Hermione

The Stanford sisters, circa 1909: Dorothy, and Eileen (seated), Alice and Helen

received a telegram from South Africa, which she opened with some trepidation. It announced: "Have worked it out: when I saw it, it was surrounded by carriages, not cars!"

She returned home an elegant young lady – an elegance she retained all her life, with the deportment to match. She had strong Stanford features, and a close resemblance to her sisters, to whom she was very close throughout her life, despite the years of education away from home.

In 1911, Dorothy married William Henry Ruffel in Stellenbosch in the Cape. Born in 1877, he was always called Harry and came from a farming family in Stebbing, Essex, in England. At the age of 15 he was employed by the railways in the London and North Western Company. (See chapter on Sir Walter Stanford for a photograph of the wedding.) Harry was the youngest of three sons, and although there were farms for each of his older brothers, Sid and Frank, there were no farming prospects for him in England.

As a result, he travelled out to South Africa to seek his fortune further afield, married and lived there for the rest of his life. He became a grain merchant, and then a saw miller.

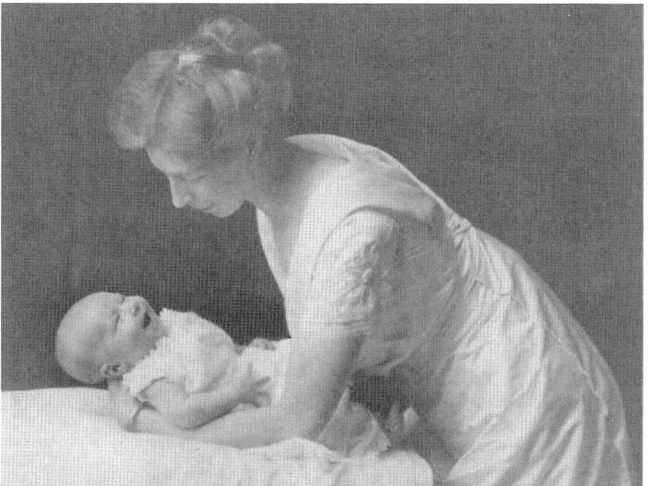

Dorothy with Edmund, 1912

The family story goes that Dorothy was very shy and that she married Harry because she felt so sorry for him when he turned up for tea one day, having been invited by Alice, her dashing and very pretty younger sister. Alice, however, had completely forgotten and gone off to play tennis, Dorothy entertained the young man while thinking up what terrible things she would say to Alice, completely forgetting to be tongue-tied in front of the unknown gentleman. He was quite charmed!

By September 1912, Harry and Dorothy were living in Bloemfontein, when Henry Edmund was born. They remained there for several years, and Lois (Frances Marjorie Lois), Tony (Anthony Stanford) and Hermione (Dorothy Elisabeth Hermione) were all born and spent their childhoods there. They rode to school on horseback, played tennis with enthusiasm, and enjoyed visits to the wider Stanford family in the Cape.

Harry was a grain broker, but sadly went broke in the Great Depression.

Ganku kept a diary from 1876 until shortly before his death in 1933, and he had been working intermittently on transforming these, together with a huge collection of letters, into a book, *The Reminiscences*. He had returned to the work in 1922 while living in Stellenbosch and was fortunate to secure the services of an amanuensis, Miss Cumming, the daughter of his close friend, Mr W.G. Cumming. When he and Alice moved to Rondebosch in 1925, this arrangement and the project ceased.

In 1927, Dorothy decided to leave her family for a time and came to her father's assistance. He began to dictate once more,

Lois and Edmund Ruffel, 1916

but Parliamentary work continued, and the demands of his philanthropic and sporting interests, as well as of his family, tended to increase rather than diminish once he was living in the city of Cape Town.

I do not know exactly how long Dorothy devoted her time exclusively to the project, but the memoirs were completed in 1929. In the Preface to the 1st volume of *Stanford's Reminiscences*, it is stated:

"In the preparation of the *Reminiscences* for publication, invaluable assistance was received from Mrs Dorothy Ruffel, Sir Walter Stanford's eldest daughter. For many years she acted as amanuensis to her father, and the bulk of the original manuscript of more than 800 foolscap pages is in her handwriting. She also supplied much of the material for the Introduction and for the Preface; arranged and catalogued the voluminous Stanford Papers, and supplied information and explanation in connection with the text."

In the 1930s, Dorothy regularly contributed articles to *The Friend*, a newspaper in Bloemfontein, for which she wrote under a number of pseudonyms: Dema (a play on her initials), Amed (…in reverse), Eave or Eavesdropper – the latter two when the article did just that! The articles all displayed wit, often a degree of subversion, and an ability to make acerbic comments on the social mores of the times. Despite her discipline in all matters of good manners and comportment, she nevertheless had the ability to be a quiet rebel. She, like her father, had a strongly held belief in the principle of African participation in government and political determination.

After their financial difficulties in the depression, Harry moved the family to Elgin in order to become the first Company Secretary of the Elgin Farmers' Cooperative. He then secured the contract to saw the timber from Lebanon Plantations for the South African Forestry Department, and founded a saw milling business, Elgin Timbers. This would eventually be run by his son, Edmund, who, in turn expanded the business to build wooden houses.

1939 saw both daughters leave South Africa: Lois to marry Jim Green in England, and Hermione, who married a Mauritian Frenchman, Roger Piat, to live in the Congo. Dorothy was an inveterate letter writer, and had to content herself for very many years with keeping in touch with her beloved daughters in this manner. Her letter-writing continued throughout her life, keeping the wider Stanford circle up to-date with everybody's 'goings on'.

Tony trained as a pilot for the South African Air Force at the outbreak of World War II. His plane was shot down in 1940 and he was forced to ditch into water. He survived 12 hours in the sea was picked up and held as a prisoner of war (POW) in Germany for the rest of the war. For several months, the family did not know if he was alive or dead, but eventually, through a coded message broadcast by the BBC, they learned of his capture and imprisonment. For the next three years, Dorothy in South Africa and Lois in

Harry and Dorothy Ruffel in 1935

England dealt with the authorities and with the Red Cross to send him parcels: a task which was achieved despite many difficulties, including the number of times he was transferred to different POW camps. Dorothy's dogged determination to send him little luxuries is evident in the exchange of letters between her and Lois, which are filled with complicated plans.

In 1949, Harry and Dorothy were at last able to visit England and see Lois and her three children: Malcolm, Frances and Celia. I remember the visit well: The smell of pipe from 'Grannypa' (my name for Harry), his scratchy tweed suit, and his gentleness and affection. I remember, too, going into their bedroom with my sister in the early mornings and watching Granny do her exercises. Clearly, she had inherited not only self-discipline and a belief in exercise, but also a lack of self-consciousness from her father!

Sadly, that was the only time I met my grandfather. He died in March 1950, having suffered poor health for a while. One of his catchphrases, no doubt caused by not feeling well, was "I am leg-weary." He was 73 when he died.

Granny 'A' (Africa – the name always used by Lois's family to distinguish her from Granny 'E',

Harry Ruffel with his granddaughter, Celia, Stonecross, Colchester, England, circa 1949

England!) survived her husband by another 29 years. During this time she frequently visited Europe, staying for extended periods with Lois in Colchester and with Hermione, then living in France. It was on one such visit to Hermione at their home in Paris – 'Chatelaine' – that a telegram from Dorothy's brother-in-law, Bill Stubbs, arrived announcing the death of her youngest sister, Eileen. Veronique was seven at the time, and Hermione and Roger were not there. The telegram had been spelt phonetically (by the French) and Dorothy could not decipher it, so she asked Veronique to interpret. As the little girl did so, she realised the import of the message and went and sat on her grandmother's lap. Veronique remembers: "Granny was crying, but was nevertheless able to reassure me and somehow imbue in me her deep belief in the unimportance of death. It was for me an extraordinarily formative experience."

During the late 1950s, and certainly influenced by her father's attempts to get enfranchisement, irrespective of race enshrined in the Union of South Africa, she joined the Black Sash movement – a non-violent white women's resistance organisation. This was founded in 1955 and campaigned against the removal of coloured or mixed race voters from the voters' roll in the Cape Province by the National Party government. As the apartheid system began to reach into every aspect of South African life, Black Sash members demonstrated against the Pass Laws and the introduction of other apartheid legislation. Between 1955 and 1994, the Black Sash provided widespread and visible proof of white resistance towards the apartheid system.

By the late 60s, Dorothy was living with her son, Edmund, at High Rising, near Grabouw, and in 1976 she decided to move to England to be closer to her two daughters. She lived her last two years with my sister,

Frances, in Colchester, spending several months each year in the Lot in France with Hermione and Roger. She was by now in her 90s, but continued to go for her constitutional walk every day; always dressed with panache, accessorising her stylish clothes with a dash of bright colour and usually a smart hat. Many of her friends in Colchester referred to her as The Duchess!!

Dorothy's 90th Birthday in England, 1976

STANDING, LEFT TO RIGHT: *James Dowson, Russell Edey, Frances Dowson, Malcolm Green and Celia Edey (grandchildren), with Anthony Edey*

MIDDLE, LEFT TO RIGHT: *Lois, Alexandra Green, D.M.R., Kate Edey, Jim (son-in-law)*

SEATED FRONT: *Nicola and Andrew Green, Julia Dowson, Philip Edey and Henry Dowson (all great-grandchildren)*

Sheila Kilpin, her niece, said of her: "Aunt Dorothy was a memorable person, tall and upright to the end. Even when family circumstances were difficult financially, she always carried things off with flair; always dressed with distinction, usually set off by a magnificent hat, which she would have made herself. Her entrances were spectacular. She kept up with all that was going on, was politically involved, and was the authority on family history, with a terrific loyalty. When a grandson fell foul of the law and was in Pollsmoor Prison (in South Africa), Aunt Dorothy was the one, who, in full regalia, would visit him every month. She was a person who influenced all of our lives."

Dorothy always behaved with dignity and courteousness. She had impeccable manners and high expectations of behaviour from all around her. Her grandchildren and great-grandchildren did not want to disappoint her, but knew she would continue to love them unconditionally, even if their standards slipped momentarily!

Veronique says of her: "Granny had a particular genius with all her grandchildren in that she was able to make each of them believe that they had a special and privileged relationship with her. I do not really know what the secret was, but it was only recently that I realised that we all thought that our own relationship with her was the most exclusive of all the grandchildren. We all kept quiet for fear of hurting the other cousins' feelings. It was a tremendous gift and benediction."

I heartily agree with this description and still feel my relationship with her was 'special'.

She died in March 1979 after a brief illness at Stonecross, Lois and Jim's home in Colchester.

Granny (Dorothy) and Celia, June 8, 1968

Robert Cecil Stanford

Robert Cecil was the next child, born to Walter and Sarah Alice in March 1889. Tragically, he died of diphtheria when he was little more than two years old.

Sarah Alice's brother, Arthur Edward Mortimer Walker (who was then aged 22) was living with the Stanfords in Kokstad at the time. He wrote in poignant detail to his mother about little Bobby's illness and death. It would appear that he was ill for at least a week, but by the time it was confirmed he had diphtheria, it was too late to save him. In the letter Arthur describes the events thus: "…We kept on steaming, hoping against hope, but it was no use; he got rapidly worse. Towards the end he suffered a great deal of pain, rolling about the bed and calling to his father in a choking whisper which could not be understood. From about ½ hour before he died up to the end, his father took him in his arms & soothed him & he seemed better for it, I mean in spirits, for it was clear to us all that he was nearing the last. His father sat on the bed with him in his arms & he passed away quietly…

"Poor old Walter, he kept up bravely, it was only as the morning dawned he came back in the room & lifted the covering from our darling. It was too much for him, he broke down then and all that long miserable cold day he went about with a hungry look in his eyes… I never saw a child with our darling's disposition & I never loved any child so much; it has been a great grief to me & what his parents have suffered you can realise. When I think of him & all his little ways, I feel as though my heart is bursting. His greeting to me every morning was "Morning Arfur"& I always loved to hear it.….I think that if Bobby had lived, he would have made a magnificent man."

Alice Minnie Stanford

Alice was born in Kokstad in 1890. I know very little of Alice's early years and education, other than sharing her childhood with her siblings, all of whom were very close and affectionate.

In March 1920, however, she married Alec Carswell Smith in Rondebosch.

My mother, Lois, is the flowergirl sitting on the right, beside Ganku

A full report of the wedding appeared in the S.A. Lady's Pictorial in March 1920:

"**Carswell Smith – Stanford.** The wedding of Alice, second daughter of Col. Sir Walter and Lady Stanford of "Monteith", Rondebosch, and Mr Alexander Carswell Smith, of Stirling, Scotland, which took place on January 29th at St. Paul's, Rondebosch, was a very popular one. The church (beautifully decorated) was crowded with a large number of guests. The Rev Dr. Booth performed the ceremony, the best man being Lieut. Prentice and the groomsman being Major Gordon. The bridal procession was particularly bright and picturesque, the bridesmaids, trainbearers and little flower-girl all wearing a pretty shade of yellow, with flowers to match the frocks.

The bride was given away by her father and looked very stately and charming in a lovely draped gown of duchess satin and ninon embroidered in silver roses. The skirt, the train and the corsage were handsomely embroidered in seed pearls and silver beads, the long narrow train of satin being lined with silver tissue and edged with tiny frills of yellow ninon. She wore a lace-edged veil and wreath of orange blossoms and carried an artistic bouquet of delicate pink and white carnations. The bride was attended by her two sisters, the Misses Eileen and Helen Stanford, who both wore fascinating frocks of pale yellow brocade made with panniers falling in points over frilly ninon underskirts. The sleeves, which were worn short, were edged with ninon frills, which again appeared on the large butterfly bows at the back, which finished off the draperies of the corsage. Large black tulle bows – instead of hats – gave a decidedly "chic" touch to the frocks. The little flowergirl (who preceded the bride into church) and the two little trainbearers were Lois Ruffel (the bride's niece), Dorothy Driver and Jean Buchanan, who looked very sweet and dainty in long "Kate Greenaway" frilly frocks of pale yellow net over silk, with crossover fichus of net and lace caps with ribbon streamers.

The service was choral; Mrs Fleetwood Nash singing a solo. After the ceremony a large reception was held at the Rondebosch Hall, which had been beautifully decorated with yellow flowers and palms.

Lady Stanford received in a smart gown of navy blue satin and ninon embroidered in gold, and a blue and gold hat. Mrs Ruffel, the bride's sister, wore a pretty frock of white georgette and lace insertions and a Leghorn hat. There were about 200 guests. The Hon. Mrs FitzRoy was gowned in white net over satin belted with blue, and a black picture hat, Mrs Carter in black crepe-de-chine, and Mrs Thorne looked well in navy-blue charmeuse trimmed with gold brocade."

Alec was born in Stirling, Scotland, in May 1892. He had a brother, James and a sister, Jean. There was a third sibling, Jenny, who died from pneumonia when she was quite young. The family farmed in Stirling, and Alec was sent out to South Africa just before World War I with horses, mostly Clydesdales. It was a pretty rough trip, and some horses were lost overboard in heavy seas, which broke his heart. James is thought to have travelled with him. Alec was a gentle giant and renowned for his strength, holding up a car to have a wheel changed and being able to carry a sack of mealies (sweetcorn) with a man on top of it!

During World War I, he fought 'up north' and contracted Black Water Fever, a complication of malaria. He was carried by bearers for some weeks back down to South Africa. A runner went ahead to advise the next village that they were bringing a very sick man through, and they would have boiled chicken and other such things to nurse him. It was because of the villagers that he survived.

He and Alice met in Cape Town at a point when Alice was considered almost on the shelf! She was 30 and he was 28 when they married. Alec was offered the job of running Tarka, outside Cradock in the Eastern Cape.

A contemporaneous report describes Tarka thus:

"The Tarka Training Farm of the 1820 Memorial Settlers' Association is specially intended to prepare settlers from overseas to take up farming in South Africa. It receives them on arrival and gives them in the least possible time an understanding of the rudiments of South African farming. Whilst so learning, the settler is also finding out on the spot whether he is really suited to farming and it to him. Simultaneously he is being tested under sympathetic and experienced hands as to his fitness for such a life, and prepared for further training with a private farmer. There is a similar institution for women, but conducted on private lines, at Harrismith in the Orange Free State.

"After the preparatory period at Tarka, settlers are assisted to gain further experience on farms as learners. In this way they gain, under kindly guidance, an insight into the practical details of different kinds of farming in several districts. Gradually they are launched as independent landowners or tenants, but only when they can commence farming on their own account, on a scale suited to their means and with every reasonable prospect of success. To the established farmers who have thus opened their homes and have given time and trouble to training them, numberless settlers owe a great debt. The knowledge that such a system exists, controlled by a local organization with representatives in Great Britain, has given and should continue to give confidence to prospective farm-settlers."

It was at Tarka that Alec and Alice's two children, Dorothy and Allison, were born (1921 and 1923) and spent their childhood. Alec had his Clydesdales there, as well as cattle, and was a judge and exhibitor at local shows. He was exceptionally good at plaiting the horses' manes. When his granddaughter, Bronwyn, was little with

long hair, she would go to him and ask him to plait her hair for a party. He was thrilled, and Bronwyn loved it, but Alice and Allison weren't too impressed!

LEFT: *Alice with Dorothy and Allison as a baby, circa 1923*
BELOW: *Uncle Alec at Tarka, 1935*

When the Royal family came out in 1942, Alec was introduced to the King, who chatted, then asked him how long he had been out from Scotland. Later, Alec asked Alice: "How did he know I came from Scotland?" The Scots never seem to lose their accent, even after many years.

In the mid-1940s, Alec and Alice moved to Pretoria, where he ran a dairy farm – Glen Farm, then owned by the Struben family but now the grounds of St Albans School. They lived in a wrought-iron Boer War farmhouse, which Bronwyn loved. She remembers that there were dairy cows named after her and her brother, Gwyn. They were always keen to see what 'our cow's' milk production was. Alec was proud of his cooling machine, which prolonged the life of the milk at the time. During the 40s, his sister, Jean, came out from Scotland with her son, Sandy, and stayed on to run the farm next door, Faerie Glen, which is now a smart suburb of Pretoria. Sandy still lives in South Africa.

Alec was wonderful at doctoring sick animals and had many old farmers' wives' potions and treatments. Many of the surrounding farmers called on him, sometimes in the middle of the night, for his help to save an animal. He always thought the best of people and was taken for a ride by many. His retirement years were difficult, but people were very generous. A friend of mine grew up on the neighbouring farm, Lynnwood, and remembers Alec and Alice with affection. Alec continued to have Clydesdales on Glen Farm, and she remembers the poignant moment when the contents of the property were auctioned off. When Alec saw the harnessing and saddlery for his horses sold, he stood with his hands in his pocket, tears running down his face. They owned a beautiful place in Swaziland for a while, then in Karkloof in Natal. Sadly, having been a heavy smoker most of his life, he died of emphysema in 1968 after years of being nursed by Alice.

Alice was definitely a Stanford woman. She was capable and talented. She was a self-taught artist who did mainly landscapes and still-life work. She was also an accomplished knitter and sewer, as was necessary when living so far from town and where so little was available 'off the shelf'.

She told the story that they were having important guests to the farm (Tarka) and that she was serving a young whole piglet. She asked the cook to put an apple in the mouth when it was served. Much to Alice's horror, cook brought the piglet in to be carved with the apple in her own mouth! Alice herself was a great cook and preserver who made full use of what was available on the farm. She, like her mother, loved gardening, and her granddaughter, Bronwyn, clearly remembers collecting seeds in the autumn for the next summer show. Alice grew white watsonias that had been collected in the Eastern Cape by her mother, Lady Stanford, and took the bulbs with her wherever she set up home. In turn, Allison also grew those same watsonias in her garden. They were nurtured in the family for over 100 years!

Alice also had a wicked sense of humour, and she and Allison would have hysterical laughs over seemingly nothing. Alice was always considered to have the neatest ankles: a great asset when they were all that could be shown in those days!

Alice and Alec loved their picnics in Tarka – perhaps because there wasn't very much else to do. A wagon would be inspanned and they'd go down to the river for the day. The Scotch cart would be used to go to the cinema in Craddock, which was another big treat. When they were young, their daughters, Allison and Dorothy, had governesses on the farm, but were later sent down by train to Rondebosch Girls School in Cape Town, close to where their grandparents, Ganku and Granny Alice, lived.

There were always cats, dogs and chickens (skippertjies and bantams) around Alice's house. When they lived in Swaziland, a veld fire had come pretty close to the house, and there had been a hen sitting on eggs in the grass as the fire crept closer. Alice was out in her nightie beating at the flames and winning the day. Her grandchildren thought this very funny to behold.

Her last years were spent living with various siblings and family members. She sewed and painted right up until the last, and her death in 1973, aged 83, was very quick and sudden.

Alice riding side-saddle

Alice starts her life-long passion for painting

Arthur Warner Stanford

Arthur was born in Kokstad in 1893. He first went to school in Cape Town at age seven, to the Diocesan College's Preparatory School, which was run by Miss Charlotte Brooke in the yard of the headmaster's old house. He then attended Bishop's, where his only claim to fame was being a member of the famous under-16 team that won one of its rugby matches against Rondebosch Boys High – 112 points to nil! At cricket, he was considered a fairly indifferent left-arm bowler, but he always retained a love and an interest in the game, which he passed on to his family.

After matriculating, he went on to the College of Agriculture at Elsenberg, attaining his Diploma of Agriculture with honours as the top student and gold medallist of his year. He won a scholarship to study veterinary science in the USA, but his family were against him going, so he never took that up. Instead, as we have already seen, when his older brother, Elliot, made the move to farming in East Griqualand, Arthur went with him (he was only 18 at the time). He lived at Inungi from 1911 to December 1914, when Elliot and Effie married. While they were away on honeymoon, Arthur left to sign up, starting with a period with the SA Field Artillery (Mounted Rifles) in South-West Africa in 1914, until the end of that campaign.

In September 1915, he married Eily Dorothy Leary, the daughter of W.P. Leary, one of the Transkei Magistrates, who had been a colleague and friend of Ganku's for a number of years. The story is that Eily sold her mandolin to pay for her train ticket down to Cape Town to marry Arthur before he set sail for England. This was done without her parents' knowledge or consent. Quite brave, really, for 1915! Ganku welcomed her to his home in Rondebosch and asked Arthur if he had proposed marriage. On hearing that this was the case, he presided over the wedding, and the marriage was conducted at St Thomas' Church, Rondebosch. W.P. Leary was a great character and spent long periods of time staying with the family at Inungi.

Arthur Warner Stanford and Eily Leary's wedding, September 1915; Ganku is in the middle of the back row

Late in 1915, after their wedding, Arthur and Eily went to England, where he was commissioned in the Royal Field Artillery. He fought in France on the Western Front from the beginning of 1916 to the end of the war. On July 1, 1916, aged 23, and a young subaltern serving in the 370th Battery, 29th Division, 4th Army on the Western Front for the opening battle of the Somme, he was sent forward as an artillery liaison officer to the second battalion of the South Wales Borderers to send messages back to his battery. Second Lt Stanford miraculously survived the hail of machinegun bullets as they went over the top. Out of that battalion of some 1 000 men, he was one of only 60 who survived being killed or wounded. His performance that day got him his first Mention in Dispatches.

Arthur Warner Stanford

While he was fighting at the Somme, Eily gave birth to their first child, Walter Power, in Cape Town on July 2, 1916.

The fighting on the Somme continued for many more weeks, and in October 1916 he was awarded an immediate Military Cross for, as the citation reads: "great courage and resource in moving a section of his Battery to a forward position under circumstance of great difficulty and heavy shell fire from the Germans. Finding it impossible to move the guns with horses, he took them to pieces and carried them on trolleys up the valley running east of Eaucourt Valley under heavy shell fire. Lt Stanford has been brought to notice on four previous occasions for gallantry and devotion to duty."

A further diary entry from the Divisional records reads: "October 30, 1916. The 13th and 92nd Battery Section (Stanford's) dismounted its guns and took them up on a light railway. This movement is described by the brigade commander as an achievement of great skill and resource. It was hardly possible to walk over much of the country."

He became a major in July 1917. In 1918 he received the Distinguished Service Order, the citation being: "This officer has commanded his Battery with great gallantry and skill and has inspired all serving under him with that spirit of loyalty and disregard for danger so essential to success in war. He has invariably displayed the greatest courage under fire and the state of efficiency to which he has brought the Battery has brought the greatest credit on him."

In 1918 he was awarded the French Croix de Guerre, which he received in June 1919, and was mentioned in dispatches three times.

Major Arthur Warner Stanford

On returning to South Africa in 1919, after a brief spell living in the hut Elliot had built for him at Inungi, he and Eily took up residence at Alwyns Poort, next to Inungi and part of the original farmlands. Their niece, Sheila Kilpin, described Eily as a difficult character, inclined to bemoan her lot in life. However, she and Arthur had three more children: Richard Ennismore, Naomi Dorothy and Marion Alice were all born in Kokstad in 1920, 1921 and 1922 respectively.

There was already a shed and some huts at Alwyns Poort, but he decided to build a new house. A furrow was made at the site from one of the strongest mountain springs, and his new house was built: A very big rondavel, 30ft in diameter. The side sections were partitioned off to form two bedrooms, and a passageway on the south side led to a lean-to kitchen and pantry. The front section was also cut off to form a stoep with a low wall – columns holding up that section of the roof. The foundations were stone and the house was approached by steps in front.

Cynthia remembers being taken by Effie to see the roof trusses raised, and she recalls the doubts expressed as to whether the walls would withstand the thrust of such a large roof span. The poles were very heavy, and she remembers one or two 'boys' were needed for each when they were lifted into position. The wall did not collapse! This only happened years later when a new owner removed the columns, which caused the roof to collapse on that side.

Cynthia Payne, another niece, remembers spending time with the family at Alwyns Poort and tells an amusing anecdote about Arthur: "At the back of the house was a place where the sods were cut out for building the house, and in the summer it got full of water. It was too muddy for bathing, so instead we took the big tin bath and made it into a boat. It was a good boat, but difficult to steer and rather wobbly. Uncle Arthur came to see what we were doing and wanted to sail, too. So he got into the bath, but when he got into the middle of the pool the boat sank and he was covered in mud and water. We laughed very much, but ran away because he was feeling fierce!"

Arthur with his sons, Walter Power, left, and Richard Ennismore, right, in 1939

They remained in East Griqualand until 1923, when they returned to the Cape to educate their children.

During World War II, Arthur was recalled from the Reserve of Officers and acted as a staff officer to Brigadier Piet de Waal at defence headquarters. He was later appointed Fire Command, Table Bay Defences, and finally OC Coast Defences, which covered all the main sea ports from South West Africa to Durban. By this time he was a Lieutenant-Colonel.

During this period, Arthur and Eily bought a small farm called Tally Ho in Elgin, where they grew apples, pears and grapes. It was a much-loved place for the family, and particularly for their grandchildren, the children of Walter Power, Dickie and Naomi. Sadly, Marianne died of scarlet fever at the age of eight.

Arthur's granddaughter, Diana, remembers him with affection. He was known to his grandchildren as Gramps or Grampie, and she remembers hearing the story of his great escape at the Somme – always told in the third person – and of him singing traditional Xhosa songs with her grandmother. Eily was an excellent pianist and spoke fluent Xhosa, collecting some wonderful traditional songs over the years.

Arthur taught them all the fielding positions in the game of cricket and how to appreciate the radio broadcasts of Test matches. He had a keen, dry sense of humour; always ironic and understated. He would tease Eily, who was quite sensitive about her cooking. She tried very hard to make things perfect, but loved compliments, so Gramps would say it tasted terrible! Everyone knew he didn't mean it, but Eily would rise to the bait every time. Diana spent a lot of time with them while she was at boarding school and came to appreciate and love them very much.

Arthur died at Tally Ho in Elgin in 1978 at the age of 85.

Helen Rose Stanford

Helen was Walter and Alice's fifth child and third daughter. Described as dashing and very pretty, she was born in Cape Town in January 1898. Although she played the piano a bit, she was more interested in the stage – especially dancing – but was discouraged from this by the prevailing view that the stage would not be a suitable career for a lady. She always regretted this lost opportunity for self-expression. She attended Rustenburg Girls' High School in Rondebosch for a time, which was within walking distance of their home, 'Monteith', in Silwood Road. Like many others in that period, Helen's education was derived more from her extensive reading than from the classroom.

In November 1924, aged 26, she married Cullis Hamilton Relly (always referred to as Hamilton or "Hammy" to distinguish him from his uncle, who was also Cullis). They met while living on neighbouring farms just to the north of Stellenbosch. She was with her parents on Lindani, and he with his Uncle Cullis on Lorraine.

Wedding of Helen and Hamilton Relly

Hamilton had been born in South Africa, but from aged seven lived in Eastbourne, Sussex with his widowed mother and older brother, Owen. Immediately on leaving school in 1916, he eagerly joined up and spent the remainder of World War I in the Royal Tank Corps. He was involved in most of the main tank battles on the Western Front. He had a number of nasty experiences and was wounded several times. Even after his marriage, Helen removed pieces of metal from his back. His interest in war books and magazines continued throughout his life. Sadly, for him, few of his own contemporaries with whom he could share experiences survived the war. However, while serving in the trenches, Hammy did some beautiful black and white sketches of the trench warfare, including some of the first tanks.

Cullis Hamilton Relly in his Cape Corps uniform

Drawn, among other things, by the sun, he returned to South Africa after the war to work with his uncle on the farm Lorraine. After his marriage to Helen, they went to London for him to start art classes. He drew well with either hand, but was unable to continue, owing to his colour blindness. (He also played tennis with either hand and therefore failed to cultivate a backhand shot!)

Once back in South Africa, they began farming at Yolani in the Constantia basin. but in 1930 moved to Waterkloof Farm, near Somerset West. According to his niece, Sheila, "Uncle Hammy pioneered the export of quality table grapes under his own 'Bantu' brand. Well known for a large-berried 'white prince' variety, his grapes were frequently served at banquets at Buckingham Palace. He called one variety he had developed 'Helena', after his wife."

Helen and Hammy had two sons, Gavin Walter Hamilton, born in February 1926, and Bruce Hamilton, born in November 1929. Bruce remembers picking, sorting and packing the grapes for transportation overseas. Waterkloof remained financially successful up until Wold War II. Sadly, after the war, individual grape brands could no longer be marketed under an individual name or brand, and the viability of the enterprise ceased.

During World War II, from 1939–1945, Hamilton served with the Cape Corps, and took convoys of vehicles containing materials and personnel through Africa to Abyssinia. Consistent with his love of nature, he was amazed at the size and markings of the butterflies he saw in the highland forests of Marsabit in Kenya. He survived malaria during this campaign.

He was a shy person and a very enthusiastic angler who loved nature – butterflies, plants, fish (not only butterflies in Kenya, but small fish in the shell holes in the battle fields of France!). Bruce remembers him as a kindly father and a practical person – always interested in sharing his special knowledge of nature

Helen Relly with Gavin

and his workshop activities. Although he didn't go to university, he attended Elsenberg College and was a well-informed and inventive farmer.

Helen doted on her boys, Gavin and Bruce, and with Hammy's support, insisted on the best for them, despite modest family resources. She read widely, was philosophically and politically liberal and supported the principles eventually espoused by the Progressive Party. She was always loving and hospitable to the nephews and nieces who visited the farm, in particular Helen Pat Stubbs, whose parents (Eileen and Bill) lived for much of the year in (then) Northern Rhodesia, which was considered to be unhealthy for her.

Helen with Bruce, left, and Gavin

Waterkloof continued to be a much-loved and much-visited home for the wider family for a long time to come. It was there that Granny Alice died in 1937.

Hamilton returned to Waterkloof to farm grapes in 1944 under the brand of the Deciduous Fruit Board (DFB). The fruit not sold for table consumption went to the KWV distillery, with its entitlement to the grower of wines, spirits and fortified wines at favourable prices. Nevertheless, Hammy was discouraged and sold the farm to a Mr Riddering in about 1965. Hammy and Helen then moved to Knysna, where they designed and built a new and comfortable home they called Pilleygreen, which overlooked the golf course and the lagoon. Hammy made another garden there, with lots of homemade compost, and went fishing in the lagoon in a small boat he had acquired. After a few years, Riddering defaulted on the purchase agreement, whereupon (about 1969) Gavin bought Waterkloof back, and his parents re-established themselves there. Gavin installed several managers in turn, including Allison Collings (née Carswell-Smith) and her husband, Douglas.

After Helen's death in 1987 and Hammy's in 1990 – both at Waterkloof – Gavin's son, Giles Relly, lived on the farm. He continued to produce grapes commercially, including the 'Helena' grape – a beautiful and luscious variant Hammy had nurtured from seeds germinated before he went off to war. Though sought after in

the local shops, they lacked consistency and durability for export purposes.

In about 2000, the farm was finally sold out of the family to winery developers, who established additional vineyards and a restaurant at the top of the farm. Apparently all of the original table grape vineyards on the lower farm have been pulled out – certainly the famous 'white prince' variant. In 2016, the estate manager turned up a World War I Tank Corps button, which certainly would have been Hammy's. It was returned to Bruce Relly.

Waterkloof Farm, Somerset West

LEFT: *Helen in a ball gown at Waterkloof*

BELOW: *A photograph used for an advertisement for the 'Helena' table grapes. The boys are Bruce and Gavin Relly. The girls are Allison and Dorothy Carswell Smith (Alice's daughters)*

Eileen Mary Stanford

The youngest of Walter and Alice's children, was **Eileen Mary**, born in Rondebosch in 1902 – so four years younger than her next sibling, Helen. Like Helen, Eileen went to Rustenburg Girls' High School in Rondebosch. In 1929, Eileen married William Frederick Stubbs (always called Bill) in Cape Town. According to Sheila Kilpin, Eileen's niece: "They met on board ship travelling from the UK to South Africa, and I remember a telegram arriving telling of their engagement, and Mom and Dad's horror (Elliot and Effie) as 'Eileen's engaged to some fellow she met on board' (shipboard romances are notoriously suspect). It was a very happy marriage, and when we were in England, we went to stay with Bill's parents outside Oxford, where Bill's mother, Mrs Stubbs, said they were so horrified when Bill announced his engagement to 'some girl he'd met on board'. Their fears were only allayed when Ganku and Granny met them on the docks at Cape Town when she came out for the wedding."

LEFT: *Bill Stubbs and Eileen, 1929*

BELOW: *Their bridesmaids and pageboy*

Report on Bill and Eileen Stubbs's Wedding

SOCIETY WEDDING AT RONDEBOSCH
Stubbs-Stanford

Yesterday afternoon, in St Paul's Church, Rondebosch, Eileen Mary, the youngest daughter of Sir Walter and Lady Stanford of Lindani, Rondebosch, was married to William Frederick Stubbs, son of Mr and Mrs Lawrence Stubbs of India. The marriage was solemnised by the Rev W.G. Webster, assisted by the Rev John Hunter.

The church had been beautifully decorated with palms, bracken and other foliage.

The bride looked very stately and graceful in a beautiful medieval frock of ivory and gold brocade. The fitting bodice was made with long, tight sleeves, and the full skirt fell to her ankles. Her waist was encircled with jewelled tassels. From her shoulders fell a long train of gold embroidered net, finished at the end with a bow and ruchings of tulle. Her full veil was held in place by a net cap bordered with gold leaves and orange blossoms. Her only ornament was a necklace of sapphires and pearls, which had been given to the bridegroom's mother on the occasion of her own marriage. She carried a bouquet of pink and apricot roses and fern.

The bridesmaid, Miss Annie Syfret, wore a frock of deep apricot ring velvet. It was cut with a fitting bodice and long, tight sleeves. The full skirt, cut in wide scallops, was longer at the back than in the front, and the velvet ... at the waist was finished in front with a bow of velvet. A band of apricot leaves and petals encircled her head, and she carried a bouquet of apricot roses and fern. The best man was Mr A.K. Garrick.

Apricot taffeta
Five little flowergirls were in attendance on the bride. They were Dorothy and Allison Carswell-Smith, Marion and Naomi Stanford (all nieces of the bride), and Sheila Maasdorp.

Their charming frocks made with short bodices and long skirts were of apricot shot taffeta, with wide collars, edged with white fur. They wore bonnets of taffeta edged with fur, and each carried a taffeta muff edged with fur and finished with a posy of flowers.

The tiny page, Master Gavin Relly, a nephew of the bride, wore long trousers of apricot ring velvet, buttoning on to a taffeta shirt finished with a wide collar of georgette.

The Reception
The reception was held at Kelvin Grove, where the rooms had been decorated with bowls of roses and autumn foliage.

Lady Stanford received her guests in a frock of navy satin marocain trimmed with embroidery in gold and oriental colours, and a navy-blue hat. She carried a bouquet of crimson roses and fern.

Mrs Stubbs, who had come from India for the wedding, wore a tailored frock of bottle-green marocain with a coat to match, and a close-fitting felt hat of the same shade. She carried a bouquet of shaded pink roses and fern.

Mrs Carswell-Smith, a sister of the bride wore a frock of rose marocain with an accordion-pleated skirt, and her close fitting hat was of beige straw.

The tables had been decorated with vases of pink roses. Later the tables were cleared away, and many of the guests danced to the music of Ray Levin's Orchestra.

There was only one toast, that of the bride and bridegroom, proposed by Colonel G.A. Morris, an old friend of the family.

Later in the afternoon, when Mr and Mrs Stubbs left for their honeymoon, the bride wore a smartly tailored frock of navy marocain under a coat of blue corded silk, with deep bolster cuffs of grey fox fur and a scarf collar. With this, she wore a brimmed hat of navy silk straw and felt.

After their short honeymoon, Mr and Mrs Stubbs will leave for their home at Namwala, Northern Rhodesia.

Bill had entered the British South African Police (B.S.A.P), and then moved to the Provincial Government in Southern and Northern Rhodesia. His final posting was Secretary of Native Affairs in Northern Rhodesia, and he was awarded the C.M.G. and M.B.E. His father, Lawrence Stubbs C.S.I., C.I.E., was Commissioner of Bareilly, United Provinces in India.

Eileen Mary Stanford

Eileen was very musical, loved children, people and animals. She was also an extremely good horsewoman and used to buy pure-bred horses and break them in. In their first posting in Namwala (now in Southern Zambia), she was able to have horses (although not when they were in Northern Rhodesia, as it was then called), and she used to go for walks with her horse, cat and dogs. Bill and Eileen were very hard-up when they were first married, and were very excited when they acquired two carpets and a gramophone! They had no wireless.

Bill and Eileen's daughter, Helen Patricia Audrey, (Helen Pat to us!) was born in Rondebosch in 1930, and for health reasons, she was left with Ganku and Granny Alice when her parents were in Northern Rhodesia. Later she boarded at Herschel school until she was 14, when the family moved to England. She spent quite a lot of time staying at Waterkloof with her aunt, Helen, and her two cousins, Gavin and Bruce.

Eileen was delicate, having been born with kidney disease, and she suffered from ill health for many years. She and Bill moved to England, where they lived until her death, in Benson, near Oxford. She died in 1963 aged 61 and Bill in 1987, aged 85. Helen Pat married an army officer, Lt-Col Peter Hendy Brazier, and their son, Julian, followed in Ganku's footsteps, becoming an MP in the UK.

Helen Patricia Stubbs

FROM LEFT TO RIGHT: *Frances, me, and my cousin Michele Piat as Helen Pat's bridesmaids*

CHAPTER VIII

A Personal Afterword

While writing about my forebears in South Africa, I was struck by many recurring characteristics, and have come to ponder the nature of inherited traits and talents. The most striking themes have been those of moral courage; of striving for fairness; and of public duty. They have been accompanied by fearlessness, whether when facing physical hardship, or when standing against prevailing opinions.

But differing talents also appear: For administration; for articulacy; for creating homes and gardens; and for letter-writing. Many of these I see directly reflected in my generation, and even in the next generation. Is it coincidence that I was a Magistrate in England for 25 years? Or that two of my children have gone into the legal profession? Or that my brother, Malcolm, a doctor, had not only a brilliant medical brain, but a talent for administration – an unusual combination?

And in South Africa, Gavin Relly, Helen's oldest son, rose to be Chairman of Anglo American and led a small delegation, which was the first from the business community to meet with the ANC leaders imprisoned during the apartheid years. That meeting proved to be influential in unlocking a process that led to the eventual abandonment of apartheid. How proud would they be: Walter, J.C. Warner, and even John Stanford – the humble emigrant who stood up for the rights of his fellow settlers in 1820?

My sister, Frances, became a dancer – a profession denied her great-aunt Helen. My niece, Nicola, became an artist, a talent displayed by many of her Stanford predecessors: Uncle Elliot, Alice Carswell-Smith, and her daughter Allison, amongst others. When Nicola was painting a portrait of me (commissioned by my husband, Russell), she told me she saw it as, in part, representing one more in a line of strong Stanford women! It is also true that the 'Stanford nose' still appears in today's generation – so it remains an enduring physical characteristic

Just as I hope my ancestors would be proud of their descendants, I am proud of those who came before me. It is a sad fact that in modern times there is a tendency to 'change' history in the light of new prevailing views and social mores, and 'colonialism' is now a disdained way of life. Those seen to be part of it are discarded, along with the damaging aspects of the historical regime. This, it seems to me, fails to recognise the moral strength Ganku must have had to stand up publicly to advocate for a universal franchise, irrespective of race, during the months leading to the Union of South Africa in the first decade of the 20th century. It is interesting to speculate on how South African history would have evolved, had he won the day!

Celia aged 10, 21 and 60, displaying the Stanford nose

Celia aged 60, by Nicola Green, her niece

APPENDIX 1

The Wider Family

The first generation – Walter Ernest Mortimer Stanford's uncles and aunts

William Stanford's second brother, **John** was born in 1812. Like his father, he was commissioned in the Rural Police. In 1834 he sold his property in Southey's location, allotment No. 5, being 68 morgen* in extent, and went as a trader to Kaffirland. He was killed at Yellowwoods on December 22, 1834, at the outbreak of the 6ᵗʰ Kaffir War. (*A morgen was a unit of measurement of land area used in South Africa amongst other places. Thought to derivate from the Dutch word for 'morning' it was approximately the amount of land tillable by one man behind an ox in the morning hours of a day.)

Mary Stanford, the youngest of the Stanford family, was born disabled and never married. While Walter lived with Joseph Cox Warner, Mary gave him some of his education, and in his *Reminiscences* he described her as his very dear aunt. "I was her only pupil, and she grounded me well in the three R's. And when, some three years later, it was decided to send me to school at Lovedale, I found myself able to take a fair place in the classes there."

She died at Joseph Cox and Matilda Warner's home in 1868.

Turning now to the siblings of Walter's mother, Joanna Rosina Warner, **Mary Jane Toye** was her older sister. She married **John Bath Staples** in 1821. They had 13 children and she died aged 80 in East London in 1885.

Next came Joseph Cox Warner (whom we have already met, as he married Matilda Stanford) and then **Caroline Elizabeth**, born in Manchester in 1818. She was married on June 8, 1836, in Fort Beaufort to **Colonel Bradshaw Daniel Bell**, who was a tradesman and auctioneer in that town. He was born in about 1815 in Enniskellan, Ireland and was not an 1820 settler. He presumably came to the country with the militia. Unfortunately, the early history of his life has not been traced, nor is it known when he came to the Cape Colony. Caroline Elizabeth died in Fort Beaufort in 1851, and Bradshaw Daniel married again in August 1858 to **Rose Wright** (Rosina), the youngest child of Joanna Rosina (née Warner) and her first husband, William Wright.

Sadly, Bradshaw Daniel Bell died very shortly after their marriage in November 1858, leaving property in Fort Beaufort and elsewhere. He did not leave a will, but his son-in-law, Samuel Henry Roberts and another were appointed by the magistrate to act in the administration of his estate. He was buried in the family plot in the Fort Beaufort cemetery, along with the graves of his first wife, Caroline Elizabeth, and son, Henry, who died aged nine months, four days. William Stanford is buried there, too. Rose Wright/Bell remarried after his death and had three children from this later marriage to Edward Cottrell: Vincent, Godfrey and Winnie.

The youngest Warner child, Elizabeth, died from smallpox at age 16 in 1836.

Sarah Alice Stanford's uncles and aunts

Benjamin Walker, born 1836, died 1897

We have very little information about the **Walker** clan (her father, Joseph (jnr)'s siblings), other than the following:

The eldest of Joseph (jnr)'s sisters was **Margaret**. Born 1828, she married William Shaw Copeland and had three children. Then came **Ellen**, who married the Rev W.G. Holford. Either they had no children, or we have no record of them. **Joseph** came next, followed by **Sarah**, who did not marry. **Benjamin** married Matilda Booth; and **John Napier** married Margaret Maria Roberts, who died in India in 1901. **William** was the next born, in 1840, and he married Katherine Brownlee, but died of wounds at Manly Flats in 1915. **Richard** married Agnes Birt, and their next son, **James**, died during the year of his birth: 1844. We have no knowledge of **Mortimer Booth** beyond his date of birth: April 25, 1846. Of the youngest in the family, **Annie Jane**, we know only the fact that she died aged 20.

Turning then to the siblings of Sarah Alice's mother (**Dorothy Walker**, née Driver): Her oldest sister was **Anne**, born in 1826 and married to Charles Griffin. **Mary**, the next, died aged five in 1832; and **Hannah** married William Haynes. **Edward Bailey** married Sarah Jane Attwell and died in 1915. Then came **Dorothy**, (see earlier in book), followed by **Martha**, who married Henry Thomas Fuller. She was born in 1837 and died in 1898. **William Robert**, who was born in 1840, married Hannah Ross and they had a daughter, Annie Thackwray Driver. He died in 1914. **Elizabeth Maud** came next, who married Walter's brother, Robert Stanford. **Thomas James** married a Miss Wainwright. **Charles (Henry) Harry** and his wife, Maria Boyce Impey, had five children. In 1880 he was Resident Magistrate in Lady Frere, and with 60 European volunteers and some loyal natives, held at bay an army of enemy impis who were attacking the little township. Both their sons, William and Henry, were educated at St Andrew's College, Grahamstown and became civil servants. The youngest Driver was **Arthur Robinson**, who was born in 1848 and married Helen Webb Peddie. It is to be noted that Dorothy Walker's daughter, Sarah Alice, married Walter Stanford, and her sister, Elizabeth Maud, married Walter's brother, Robert. Put another way, Maud's niece became her sister-in-law!

The second generation

Walter's half-siblings (the children of his mother, Joanna Rosina and Capt. William Wright)

William Wright jnr was born in about 1834, and died in Queenstown on May 2, 1910. In 1873 he was appointed Resident Magistrate with Gangelizwe, and in March 1876 he became Magistrate at Emjanyana, and subsequently Chief Magistrate of Tembuland Proper, and Civil Commissioner of the Colony. He married Edith Charlotte Wynne and they had 10 children.

Mary Jane Wright was known as Mimi, and married Louis Antoine Chabaud in 1859. His father had emigrated in Wilkinson's party on the *Amphitrite,* the party's location being on the Blaaukrantz River and called New Essex. Louis Antoine became Inspector of Native Territories.

Rose Wright married first Daniel Bradshaw Bell, who was the widower of Caroline Elizabeth Warner, her aunt, but they had no children. Her second marriage was to Edward Cotterill and they had three children.

It is remarkable to note that at one time, Walter Ernest Mortimer himself was Chief Magistrate of the Transkeian Territories; his elder brother was Assistant Chief Magistrate based at Kokstad; his younger brother was Assistant Chief Magistrate based at Umtata; and his half-brother was Chief Magistrate of Tembuland Proper. At the same time, their brother-in-law, Louis Chabaud, was the Inspector of Native Territories. Joanna Rosina, their mother, must indeed have been a formidable woman to have brought her sons up with the ability and ambition to do so well in the world of administration and justice in the Native lands.

Walter's first cousins

We have already seen that after Joanna Rosina Stanford (Walter Ernest Mortimer's mother) was widowed for the second time, she and her children – three Wrights and three Stanfords – lived mainly with her brother, Joseph Cox Warner. Walter and his brothers would, therefore, have known their Warner first cousins extremely well. Throughout his life and career, Walter would have been in contact with them, not least because both **Henry Blacker** and **Ebenezer Joseph Warner** remained in the general area of the Transkei, and both were involved in missionary and administrative work all of their lives.

Henry Blacker Warner (born 1832) and **Ebenezer Joseph Warner** (born 1834) were both born in Hopewell, Natal, but in 1834 their father, Joseph Cox Warner, was appointed, with Rev Haddy, to form the Clarkebury Mission Station.

The two boys were educated on the various mission stations where their parents were sent. There were few other white people or children and they, like their father, became proficient in the Xhosa language. There was considerable unrest among the black tribes during their childhood and youth.

When Henry Blacker was about eight years old, the family were moved to the Imvani Mission Station; and when he was about 13, to the Haslope Hills Station. After the war of 1846, they relocated to Lesseyton, near Queenstown. In 1852 his parents moved to Glen Grey.

He entered the Civil Service and spent all of his service years in Idutywa in the Transkei. In 1870, he decided to resign from the Civil Service, thus surrendering his prospects of promotion and the certainty of a pension in old age in order to become a missionary.

Henry had cause to write frequently to Walter during 1894

The Clarkebury Mission Station

and 1895, on paper headed: "Office of Resident Magistrate", posted from Fort Donald.

Latterly, Henry and his wife, Elizabeth, with her sister, Emily, and two of their sons, Ebenezer and William Taylor, lived at Gwadu and also at Fort Malan with Joseph Claridge Warner, another of their sons. Henry, his wife, Elizabeth, her sister, Emily and their son, Ebenezer, were all buried in a small cemetery near Fort Malan, although there are no tombstones. Henry had apparently expressed a wish to be buried in that cemetery. Henry died in 1919 at age 87.

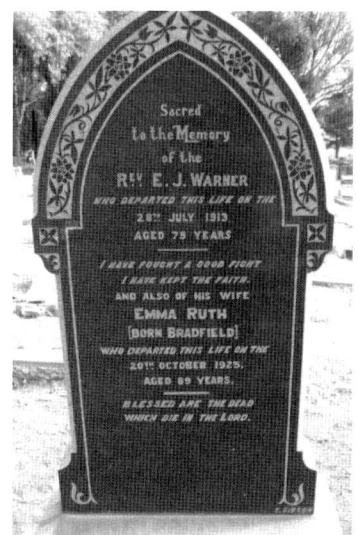

In 1852, when **Ebenezer Joseph Warner** was 18, his father became Government Agent and was put in charge of the resettling of the Tembu tribe in the Glen Grey district. It was while living there that he married **Emma Ruth Jenkins Bradfield** at Bongolo on October 15, 1859. Emma's grandfather, an undertaker, and his wife were also settlers from the period 1820–1826. Her mother, Mary, married Thomas Jenkins who had arrived as a settler, aged 13, in Shepton's party, on *Aurora*, travelling in the care of James Kidd.

Ebenezer was first appointed clerk to the Resident Magistrate for Kaffraria, now a division of King Williams Town. From there, he was appointed Superintendent of Natives at Poplar Grove, about 20 miles from Queenstown. Ebenezer and Emma were living in Clarkebury when their first son, Clarence Jenkins Warner, was born in 1860; and their second son, Harry Bradfield Warner in 1862. They probably moved to Mount Arthur after that. Their daughters, Matilda Stanford Warner and Emmeline May Warner, were born in Mount Arthur, and their next two children, Joseph Selwyn Warner and Walter Ernest Warner, were born in Queenstown. In 1870, he, too, decided to resign from the Civil Service to become a missionary.

Emma Ruth Warner

Their youngest son, William Stanford Warner, was born at Mount Arthur in 1872, and the two youngest girls, Eliza Mary Warner and Mary Maud Warner (born 1877), were both born at the mission station in Butterworth. After Ebenezer retired, they moved to a house in or near Queenstown, called Bradville. Their nieces described Emma as a "charming, gentle old lady". Ebenezer Joseph Warner died in Queenstown in 1913, aged 79, and his wife, Emma Ruth Jenkins Warner, died there, too, in October 1926.

Of Henry Blacker Warner and Ebenezer Joseph Warner's sons, five entered the Civil Service in the Native Locations Department: Clarence Jenkins Warner; Charles Edward Warner; Harry Bradfield Warner; William Taylor Warner; and John William Stanford Warner.

Sarah Alice Stanford (née Walker)'s siblings

Alice had 10 siblings, five sisters and five brothers. Two of her sisters, **Ellen Margaret** and **Anne Kathleen** died in early childhood. **Dorothy Ann**, who was born in 1855, married John George Mackenzie, had three children and lived until she was 87. **Maud Allison** was born in 1863, but I have no further information about her. **Ethelwyn May** was born in 1869 and married Thomas Stretton Barry. They had three children and she, too, lived to be 87.

The oldest of Alice's brothers was **Joseph Benjamin Walker**, born in 1861, who was said to have brought disgrace to the family, despite being adored by his nieces and nephews who called him Uncle Ben. According to Sheila Kilpin (née Stanford), one of his great-nieces, when he had a job with a firm in Port Elizabeth, he embezzled!

"His father, Joseph, bailed him out and got him another job, but he again embezzled and was then sent to Kokstad to his brothers, Arthur and Norwood, and to his brother-in-law, Walter Ernest Mortimer.

"Ben was sent to look after a farm in the valley where Walter (Ganku) ran some cattle and horses, which was supposed to be 'away from temptation'. In due course, Ganku went out to see how things were. Ben was glad to see him, but when Ganku asked how the stock was, Ben said: 'What stock?', and stock there was none! He must have sold it to the natives.

"Up with this, the magistrate and the local law firm could not put, and Ben was sent back to Port Elizabeth. His father had died (I think of shame), and Ben spent the rest of his life devotedly and efficiently looking after his mother, Dorothy. The puzzle was that no-one ever knew what he did with the money, as he didn't gamble, drink or womanise. I like to think he used it for charitable purposes. He was such a nice person."

Arthur Edward Mortimer Walker

Arthur Edward Mortimer Walker was the next brother, born in King Williams Town in May 1869. He left school at an early age, as the family faced strained financial circumstances after his father's business ventures failed. His first job was working for the law practice of Innes & Elliot in Port Elizabeth. He eventually served articles with the firm and qualified as an attorney.

By June 1891 he was living in Kokstad and working for Zietsman & Leroux. Arthur's decision to go to East Griqualand seems to have been influenced by the fact that his sister had married Walter Stanford (Ganku), the Chief Magistrate of the Transkei, and was living in Kokstad. He was able to live with them for a time.

In 1893, Arthur left Zietsman & Leroux and went into partnership with Edward Jones, to form the business Jones & Walker. Jones made his mark on history when he questioned the legal validity of a proclamation issued by the Governor of the Cape. In the late 1890s, Arthur moved down to Port St Johns to open a branch office for the Mthatha-based legal firm of Blakeway & Leppan. While living in Port St Johns, he married Kate Forbes Cumming in Somerset East in 1899. Kate had grown up in Somerset East, but would travel to Kokstad to spend holidays with her uncle, the Magistrate W.G. Cumming. At the end of 1899, they moved back to Kokstad, and Arthur returned to Zietsman & Leroux in January 1901. In August of that year, he started his own practice in a building next to A.H. William's in Main Street. It seems that Arthur later rejoined Jones for a brief period, until the formation of Elliott & Walker in 1902.

How this partnership came about is a local East Griqualand legend. Walker's former partner, Mr Jones, had died, and he and Drummond Elliot had both attended the funeral. Arthur's niece, Gyneth Walker, writes: "Mr Elliot and Mr Walker both attended Mr Jones's funeral and happened to walk back into town together. It was probably during this course of conversation, I imagine, that Mr Elliot sympathised with Mr Walker on the untimely death of his partner and then tentatively enquired if he had yet made any plans for the future. Then, having found that he had not, Mr Elliot asked Mr Walker if he would consider joining him, which apparently he did."

Arthur's son, Brian joined the firm in 1938, a year after his father's death on May 5, 1937, and remained there until his retirement in 1973. There was, therefore, a Walker in the firm for 71 years. In 2012, Milner Snell said in *A Beautiful Country*, his book about East Griqualand: "The one constant through all of the changes of the 20th century was that Elliot & Walker has continued to draw up wills and marriage contracts, and the partners have continued their weekly pilgrimages to court and still continue to dispense legal advice to the people of East Griqualand."

The next brother was **William Holford Mortimer**, who was born in 1871, married Beatrice Jane Wilson, had three children and died in 1951. He was followed in 1873 by **John Norwood Mortimer** who, according to Milner Snell, was also born in England, where his parents had gone to live for a period. They returned to South Africa when he was a baby, and he grew up in Port Elizabeth and went to school at Pearson High School and Grey College.

He worked briefly for a shipping firm in Port Elizabeth before joining his brother, Arthur, in Kokstad, where he was bookkeeper at Elliot & Walker. Norwood married Marguerite (Rita) Thomas, who had also been born of South African parents living in England. She had been a sickly child, and the doctor warned her parents that she would not survive another winter, so she was sent to her grandparents in the Cape. She was raised in Mowbray; her mother occasionally visiting from England. She and Norward had three children, and he died in 1947, but she lived to the age of 77 dying in 1957.

Harold Mortimer, the last of Joseph and Dorothy's children, was born in Port Elizabeth in 1878. He married Dorothy Cleverly and had two children. An engineer, he died in Kimberley in 1918.

A later family snap
STANDING FROM LEFT: *Arthur Stanford, Hamilton Relly, Lois Ruffel, Harry Ruffel, Tony Ruffel*
SEATED FROM LEFT: *Alice Carswell-Smith, Effy Stanford, Helen Relly, Elliot Stanford, Dorothy Ruffel, Eily Stanford*
ON GRASS FROM LEFT: *Hermione Ruffel, Dickie and Naomi Stanford*

More about Ganku

While researching this book, I spent some time at UCT in their special collections library, looking at documents archived in the "Stanford Papers BC 293". Sadly, it was not enough time to do the collection justice, but I am including in this section a few items to give a flavour of the wonderful and diverse documents available. He was a prodigious letter-writer, and there are many epistles to both his mother, Joanna Rosina, and to his wife, Alice.

BC293 B1.1

Southey Tille

My dear Mother,

I shall not be able to write you a long letter this time, but what news there is, is very bad, and it will seem the more so to you, as you did not even know that poor Aunt Mary was ill, when I tell you that she is no more. She died the day before yesterday in the morning, at about ½ past two o'clock, of heart disease. It came on very suddenly at the last, in fact we were none of us there, so it must have been doubly hard for her to die with hardly a single friend near.

Ebenezer, when he heard that she was worse, rode over, but it is fully 30 miles and when he got about half way he met a boy who was coming to say that it was all over and that our poor Aunt had breathed her last that morning. Ebenezer still went on and got to Glen Grey early. Mr Barrett and I followed the same day, but did not get there till about 9 o'clock at night. Uncle rode over yesterday morning. Doctor Kranz had been there the whole afternoon, and stopped all night. When he got there, Aunt was still walking about but he immediately ordered her to bed and told her that he would like to take her in to Queenstown with him in the morning so even he did not seem to anticipate such immediate danger although he told Uncle Charles that everything would depend upon how she slept that night. The Doctor sat up some time and then went to lie down on the sofa leaving Mrs William Wakeford who was sitting up in the room. Mrs W was sitting on the bed and Aunt lying with her arms round her neck, had been thanking her for her kindness and asked her to kiss her. After this Mrs Wakeford thought she went off into a doze and gently unclasped her arms so as not to wake her but after a little while startled at not hearing her breathe called the Doctor but she was already gone. The doctor left a paper stating that she died of Disease of the Heart and that her last words were

> *"O cherish thee*
> *God is near thee"*

and also saying that her end was peace.

The funeral took place yesterday and she was buried at the top end of the new garden, close to where Uncle Charles's little boy was buried. I have not the heart to write anything more. Goodbye. Love to all

Your ever affectionate son
WEM Stanford

BC293 B2.2

Fort Donald
23rd Nov 1874

My dearest old wife,
I am writing to you now from the Tsiki country, and tomorrow we go into Pondoland, but not for the first time as today we rode to the scene of someone's murder (into which we have to inquire) and inspected the locality.

We halted at the Kraal of one Itsundwana, a Pondo, and opened the ball by 'pumping' him about it all. Our beginning was not very promising. O'Connor asked whose kraal is this? Why do you ask? said the Pondo. That is not an answer replied O'Connor. Well, who are you asking me who I am? was the next remark of our able friend. Notwithstanding this bad start such was the affect of the insinuations and pleasant manners of the two "commissioners" that half an hour afterward we were comfortably squatted round a portly basket full of excellent Kafir beer brought us by the 'inkosikazi' of the place and ... related a full account of the murder, which I have no doubt will materially assist our inquiry. We made jokes and left that kraal high in the esteem of its proud owner. If you knew Fort Donald, it would not be necessary to tell you that it is raining. This is the place where it rains almost every day and the mists are always round the hill on which the fort is built. We are staying with Mr Davis, a trader. His wife is a nice-looking, bright little woman who was in France for five years and appears to have picked up a touch of French vivacity. She is a very kind little lady.

The poor horses are having a bad time in all of this wet and muck.

Nunqikela has written to ask for the inquiry to be postponed to Thursday next. This means a couple of days waiting, which I do not relish at all. I am wishing every day that I were at home again. I hope you are sleeping and feeling better than when you wrote last. It makes me all the more discontented when I imagine you are not well and happy.

We intend to go to Emfundiswani tomorrow: Mr Hargreaves' station, where I hope to get that letter you addressed to his care.

O'Connor has constituted himself my nurse and looks after me very well and kindly, and I am feeling as right as possible now, and intend to begin getting fat soon. We are pulling nicely together and he makes a lively companion.

We are going to dine with Mrs Sampson this evening. She is the lassie Brownlee is engaged to and is a good fellow. I asked Mrs Brownlee about the wedding picnic tragedy in Thomson's book. She said it was imaginary – although taken partly from the massacre at Nabcum in 1880.

When I began, I thought I had nothing to talk to you about, and I see I have had quite a long conversation – all on one side though – which is certainly not so pleasant as when you are present to take your share.

I hope all is going well at home. I can't say I am sorry you miss me – but you must be brave my dearest and make the best of things. Thomas and Nitu are all right. Give my love to Mound and give the children a kiss from me – wish I could just pop in on you all. Love and kisses from your very old darling

Your affectionate husband
Walter

BC293 and B202.18

Extracts from letters to Walter Ernest Mortimer Stanford from his mother written out in Granny's (Dorothy's) hand, circa 1894/5

13th May

I did not know how very ill your dear little Arthur had been till we got Effie's letter. She said he had to be steamed two nights, poor little fellow. You and Alice must have had an anxious time. The Kokstad climate seems hard on children .–

We have been greatly indebted both to you and William (William Wright: Walter's half-brother), he has helped more or less ever since he went into the police and helped your father in his sickness and sorrow. My dear sons have been very kind (especially yourself) and God has blessed and prospered them all. They are all in very comfortable circumstances.

I have it impressed on my mind that all are not willing to usifru the small portion that should come to them at my death. I wish you would write freely on this subject. I do not like the will at all, and I would rather that the property should be divided than that the will should take effect. The houses are very badly built, and often in need of repair.

With very much love dear Walter to yourself and Alice. I remain your loving

Mother

2nd July

I hear that you are appointed the head of a Commission to enquire into Sigcau's conduct since the Annexation. Though you did not tell me, I think he is being used very badly and Mr Hargreaves is grieved about it. However better that one man suffer than the whole Nation. What do you think the Government will do with him? You must have a lot of worry and anxiety with one thing and another. My poor boy, I hope your health will not fail. I would give much to spend a week with you. Love to dear Alice and the children.

9th August

Do you think Sigcau will behave more wisely in the future? He has had a hard lesson. Mr Rhodes can't always do as he wishes it seems. Are you having more rest and comfort now? Rose told me that you are very thin, but looking well, she says you have such nice lovable children, and little Arthur is very pretty like dear Bobby.

We are having pleasant warm weather but no rain .I fear we shall have a dry spring. I did not forget my dear son's birthday. May you live long and happily. Much love to dear Alice and the children and lots for yourself.

21st August

You were just going to Pondoland when Rose left Kokstad ,but I suppose you have returned by now. She arrived by train on Monday morning and the first news she was told was that her horse was lost – he had been lost a week and was knee-haltered. I thought surely he must be stolen. But fortunately a policeman brought him the same afternoon. He was found twenty nine miles on the road to his first his dearest home! Which he will never forget! This is the third time he has gone off in the same direction Rose must either sell him or keep him in the stable. I see Mr Jenner is sent to Pondoland. What does that mean? Are you relieved of all responsibility or is it a slight on you? At any rate you have enough work and travelling about without superintending Pondoland. I hope you will be at liberty to take more care of your health. You are not strong & must treat yourself accordingly. I am very anxious about my dear son and often wish if I could see you sometimes and have a long talk, and put my weary head on your shoulder. I am glad Rose stayed with you a few days, she has told me so much about your house and family, Alice was so kind and you have dear good children, and the little one is such a pretty little fellow.

Connie has passed the exam for the theory of music & is going in for the practical part , which seems to be a great trial to her. A professor is coming from England to examine the girls – and she will have to play several difficult pieces with him looking at her. She is quite nervous about it which will be against her.

31st August

There was a good deal of news in the Kokstad paper, the Editor seems to think it quite unnecessary to have sent a Special Commissioner to settle Pondoland when all disputes had been so peaceably settled before he arrived. One would think that he is just sent to Flagstaff to spy on Siqcau to bring him into trouble again. I fear this new arrangement will make things disagreeable for you (let me know) – –

Thank dear Dorothy for her nice little letter. I will write to her next week.

18th April

What a dreadful year this is. One never takes up a paper but to read of murders and terrible accidents. I am always very glad to hear from you .and especially so in these unsettled troublous times. I fear you are having a deal of worry and anxiety, for there are rumours that the Eastern Pondos are restless and dissatisfied. But I suppose that as Mr Jenner lives so near the Great Place, he would report to Government if they were likely to rebel. If the other tribes are not relieved of some of their grievance and that aggressive Glen Grey Act repealed, they will give trouble sooner or later, it is nothing better than slavery."

Amongst the collection are a great number letters of congratulations on the occasion of Walter receiving his KBE (Knighthood) in 1919. This is one example:

From: Major van Ryneveld,
Ingleside, West Hall
Grahamstown
20/06/1919

Dear Sir Walter,
Just a line to send you our hearty congratulations on your receiving the order of Knighthood, which you so richly deserved. I can't tell you how pleased I was when it was announced and I hope you will live for many years to enjoy

the same. I can quite understand how heartily sick you must be of the recruiting business. It is worrying work at the best of times, but much more so when one is surrounded by a crowd of miserable Nationalists. However, we have pulled through alright and I only hope the politicians in the old country won't now make a mess of it. I thoroughly enjoyed reading Lloyd George's reply to Hertzog. They have got it in the neck properly. You may rest assured the backrelief boer will never be given the true version of what has happened. Lies and intrigue are dished out to the unfortunate people, and they are kept in the dark as to the true state of affairs. My only son Neil is still in France. He is a Major in the R.F.A. I was very anxious for him to remain in the Army but he wishes to go farming. He is only 23 now, and but for the war was to have been at an agricultural college either out here or in America. However, he must make the best of the lost time, as many others in the same position will have to do.

I hope you are all well at home and with best wishes from Mrs van Ryneveld and self.

Yours v. Truly
Van Ryneveld

BC293 and B213.2

The collection also contains some amazing hand-illuminated manuscripts that were presented to Sir Walter at various times. The following is one example:

Front Cover   *Back Cover*

Inside pages

Stories Written by Walter Elliot Stanford (Uncle Elliot) for his great-grandchildren (1884-1989)

They belong to Margaret Gant, (née Kilpin), daughter of Sheila (née Stanford), who was the oldest daughter of Walter Elliot Stanford. I am grateful to Mickey, who gave me permission to include them.

I was naughty and did not obey my parents so my father gave me paddy whacks on my legs with a switch. I think all naughty little boys should get paddy whacks – and little girls too, perhaps. I beat my children a little bit and look how good they are – they are very good to me.

When I was small my father used to hold me in front of the saddle. When I was bigger I rode by myself.

Then later on I had my own pony which could tripple very fast.

We had a lovely deerhound named Lassie. There used to be a pair of bushbuck horns lying about and I thought it would be nice for Lassie if she had horns like other animals, so I got some string and tried to fasten the horns on to her head. She would not stand still and I got angry and smacked her. But I couldn't get the horns to stay in place. It was a great disappointment. But I think Lassie was glad as she would not have known what to do with the horns.

----oOo----

Then we went by ship from Durban to Port Elizabeth to stay with my grandparents at Hamilton House.

My cousin Ronald and I got some pieces of string and laid them out on the ground, then we prayed that they would turn into snakes. One piece of string just started to move at one end. We both saw it, and so we prayed all the harder, but nothing more happened. It was a great disappointment.

We decided that snakes were not a suitable subject for prayer.

----oOo----

I had not seen coal before and did not know what it was. They told me it was to burn instead of wood. So I took a piece of coal and box of matches and tried to get the coal to burn, but it would not catch alight. It was a disappointment.

When I stayed with my cousins in Uitenhage, we tied a long piece of string to the end of a neck tie. Just when it was beginning to get dark, we put the neck tie in the street and we pulled it across in front of anyone walking along the street from behind a hedge where we hid. People walked along the street in those days because there were no motors. Some people shrieked and ran away, some tried to hit the 'snake' but it always got away.

----oOo----

We were standing in front of the house early in the morning when my Uncle Harold walked past in his pyjamas. As he went beyond us, I saw that he had a tear in the back of his pyjama trousers so I called out: "You have got a hole behind". He turned round and said: "So have you." I did not have a tear in my trousers, so why did he say that?

----oOo----

There used to be a lame man who had to turn the points somewhere on the railway line to Uitenhage. It was difficult for him to get there because he was so lame, so he taught his tame baboon to turn the points so that the train would not get on to the wrong line. The baboon did other work as well. It used to fetch wood. But the poor baboon never got paid any money for its work. It couldn't even wear a pair of trousers because of its tail. But it got well fed and didn't have to eat horrid goggas like scorpions and centipedes.

----oOo----

I was staying at Umfundiswini with the Rev Hargreaves when Sigcau was collecting his army nearby to fight Umhlangazo. Bobbie Hargreaves and I used to go and watch as each tribal impi arrived. They approached singing their war song and the imbongi jumping about in front, shouting the praises of the chief. Then they halted and altogether gave the royal salute "Jongilanga". It was all very thrilling. Sigcau knew who we were and once put his arm on my shoulder and spoke to me about my father for whom he had a great regard. He cheated Umhlangazo and drove his forces over the border into East Griqualand where… (one line of writing missing). This was before the Annexation of Pondoland.

----oOo----

Mr John Scott was a very clever man. He knew everything and could fix anything that went wrong. He made all sorts of useful things as presents for his friends. If anybody's roof leaked he would climb up and mend it with his soldering iron.

He was very kind to me and made me a beautiful wooden wagon. I had a tame goat, and my friend Charlie and I tried to inspan the goat to the wagon but it was difficult to inspan it to one side of the disselboom. At last we got it fixed. But then the goat stood still and refused to move, even when we smacked it.

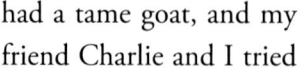

A Griqua man came past and I asked him to help us. He tied up one of the goat's front legs and then it went, but all the fastenings came loose and the goat ran away with pieces of rope hanging from it. It was a great disappointment! (Many years later when I horse jibbed, I remembered what the Griqua had done to the goat and I used the same method successfully).

----oOo----

Life was full of disappointments.

The Government built a new big house for us above and beyond the other houses. There used to be a tame wattled crane about the place, and when the prisoners went with the Scotch cart to get ant heaps for the tennis court, the crane always acted as a policeman and went along with them. One day it chased

Dorothy and Netta and they fell into the big sloot which supplied the town with water and they got very wet.

I had a pony that could tripple very fast. It could gallop very fast too. My father used to play polo on it.

Sometimes on Saturday mornings we would ride to a bathing pool in the river. Sometimes we rode out to a neighbouring farm where we would be given tea and bread and butter, or perhaps fruit. One day as we were cantering along on the way home, there was a ringhals *(a very poisonous snake)* standing up in the middle of the road. It was right in front of Ted Dalgetty's horse. The horse stopped suddenly in front of the snake and Ted shot over its head and over the snake, which got such a fright that it ran off to the side of the road. I wonder what would have happened if Ted had landed on top of the snake!

----oOo----

There used to be unoccupied… at the top end of Kokstad, which was surrounded by sod walls. These walls made wonderful hurdles and my friend Jack and I used to jump our ponies over them riding bareback.

----oOo----

We had been to visit the Rennies at Mpatoom. There was no room for me in the cart and I had to travel on the luggage rack at the back of the cart. I got bumped off at the top of church hill and knocked the funny bone in my elbow and could not use that arm to get back on to the rack. So I had to hold on to the rack and run behind the cart all the way down the hill until my arm recovered. The cart was not travelling very fast, so I was able to jump on to the rack again.

----oOo----

Some of us rode up to get evergreen for Xmas decorations at the bush on Mt. Currie. We off saddled our horses and left them to graze while we walked up to the bush where the evergreen was. When we got back there were no horses – they had run away home and we had to walk three miles carrying our saddles and dragging our sacks of evergreen.

-----oOo-----

Sometimes we borrowed our Father's sticks and played polo. Jock had an older cousin named Robin who had a very uncertain temper. When he was trying to hit the ball Jock and I hooked his stick and he flew into a rage and Jock and I had to fly for our lives. We raced up the streets of Kokstad with Robin in hot pursuit with his stick raised aloft. He didn't manage to catch up with us before we reached our homes.

----o0o----

Sometimes we did stick fighting, like Kaffirs do with two sticks. I liked doing this when I could beat the other boy.

----o0o----

The Rev Yates on his priestly rounds took a short cut across the Cedarville flats. When he came to the Umgenninuber River, it was full, so he tied his clothes on to the saddle, keeping only his hat. Then he and the horse swam across the river.

The grass on the other side was so prickly that he could not walk on it. He tried to get to his horse by throwing his hat in front of him and jumping on it. But this frightened the horse and it ran away. Fortunately somebody saw him and came to his rescue. I could not draw him any nearer, it would have been rude.

----o0o----

Many years later, I, too, took a short cut across the flats. It was winter and the water was only about 18 inches deep in the river and very cold. At the further bank was a sloping footing of clay then a steep sand slope. I took the clay obliquely and my horse's hoofs sank into it. He was a young horse and panicked and fell over sideways into the river. My leg was pinned under him and my head was under water. By leaning forward and pressing on his neck I got my head above water but that pushed his head under and he brought it up with a jerk and my head went under. I don't know how long this see-saw business went on. Finally with a frantic effort he got free and we both climbed up the bank. I had to spend an hour drying my clothes… *(bottom of page missing)*

----oOo----

Bishop Key was a large portly man. He did the rounds of his diocese on horseback, leading a pack horse with his belongings. On one occasion when he was setting forth, his curate begged to be allowed to accompany him. So

the Bishop let him lead the pack horse. The curate was not a good horseman and he lagged behind, so he had to gallop to catch up. But he could not stop in time. He had fastened the leading rein on to his saddle as he had got tired of holding it. He passed the bishop on one side and the pack horse on the other side and swept the bishop over his horse's head.

The bishop was very angry and sent the poor curate back home. He continued his journey leading the pack horse himself.

----oOo----

118

Our guests had to leave, and the river was full so they and the cart went across on the cable and the horses had to swim. The two wheelers swam across, but the two leaders ran away. I caught them and led them to the river and said: "Now you two devils are going in." As we approached the bank they speeded up, closed in against each other, lifted me off my feet and carried me into the river between them. Even if it had been planned they could not have carried it out so efficiently. If horses could laugh, they would have laughed.

----oOo----

The shearers received a sheep for every 1 000 they sheared. I had almost finished shearing and they had just one of the legs of mutton left. This had been cooked and was hanging on the wall outside the kraal. Bikwana, the local lay preacher came along past it and into the kraal. He politely greeted me, then had a chat with the shearers, then went out again. Then his head appeared above the Kraal wall and he said to the shearers: "Let us say grace." The shearers dropped their shears and piously held their hands over their eyes. Bikwana then went and cut himself a slice of mutton. That was so nice that he cut another slice and so on until there was very little meat left. His head then appeared again and he said: "Let us give thanks"! The shearers again piously complied.

He then mounted his horse and continued on his journey!

----oOo----

It had rained and if I did not get the wool across the river before it got too full, I would not have any money. The river was rising rapidly. We finished shearing and sewed up the last bales as quickly as we could, then loaded the wagon. We tied the bales on fastening the ropes to the rails. A span of oxen was waiting already inspanned and we hurried to the drift 2½ miles away. There was another span of oxen waiting there to be hitched on in front. Then we entered the river. I led the way on horseback with a rein which the *voorlooper* held so that he could withstand the current and keep the front oxen from drifting down. Each span had its driver and they swept their long whips over the oxen and shouted their names: "Ringhals, Romaan, Swartland" and the oxen knew their names and pulled as hard as they could, although they were almost on tiptoe. Then when the front oxen got to the far side, all was well. We had got the wool across and the wagon went off into Kokstad, where the wool was sailed to Durban and sold by auction to buyers from England and France and Japan.

----oOo----

I made a boat, quite a nice boat, of yellowwood. I always wanted to sail, so I stepped a mast and fixed a big sail, and Sheila (10 years old) and I sailed up the river right up round the bend to *Valschfontein*. There were not so many willow trees along the banks as there are now.

We sometimes ferried black travellers across the river when it was full. Cynthia rowed three elderly Bhasa men across. They were terrified and clung on to the sides of the boat. One of them expressed their feelings – "See how this child knows how to drive the boat. Hasn't she got a … (courage) and we sit here shivering with fright and no more use than baboons"!

----oOo----

The river was very full and overflowed into the shallow pan. Tus (8 years old) and John (4 years) were paddling in top end of this pan. At the other end was a narrow channel leading to a lower deeper pan. Somehow John got caught in the swift current of this channel. Tus shrieked for help then dashed in. Only John's head was showing, but she managed to grab him before they would both have been swept into the muddy waters of the lower pan.

----oOo----

When John and Phil were small and had to go somewhere or other, the river was full and it was before we had a boat, so they had to swim across. I was rather worried as they were very small, but they managed all right. I swam one horse across and led the other with their clothes tied on to the saddle.

----oOo----

In those days yellow Sittelana peaches grew everywhere and there was no fruit fly. So everybody could have as many peaches as they liked. Along some sod walls were quince hedges. When peaches were young, before the pips got hard, one could stick a peach on to the end of a pointed quince switch and fling it a long distance. Part of the roof of the Dalgetty's house had a coping wall along each side, and we hid behind the wall and threw peaches at passersby when they were quite a long way off and could not see where the peaches came from. They thought people hiding in the trees threw them and they got very angry. We thought it was very funny but it was very naughty and I don't think I should have told you about it. Colonel Dalgetty would have been very angry if he had known. He had been in the Indian Mutiny and was a very fierce man and he had a big nose. Mrs Dalgetty had quite a big nose, too. But she was kind to us, so I will not draw her nose. The children did not have big noses.

----oOo----

When I was a student I used sometimes to have to travel by postcart from Umtata to Cala to catch the train to Cape Town. The postcart was a large two-wheeled Cape cart drawn by six horses. There were relays of fresh horses every 16-18 miles. The driver Solomon knew I could drive and used to hand over the reins to me. In those days road repairs were done by gangs of natives (specially convicts) with picks and shovels and Scotch

carts. I was driving full trot down the Cala cutting and as we came round a bend there, a little way off, was a Scotch cart and four oxen right across the road. Solomon jammed on the brake and I pulled on the reins for all I was worth, and with the wheelers holding back in their breeching, we came to a stop with the leaders bunched up against the oxen.

----oOo----

Derick used to buck, but he only threw me off once and that was because the girth came loose.

----oOo----

Wasp was a wonderful polo pony. One scarcely needed to use the reins. One day we were out riding. John was on Wasp. A hare got up in front of Wasp, and Wasp was after it like a flash just as if it was a polo ball. It dodged about and he followed till it got away in some long grass. John was only a small boy and he had to hang on for all he was worth.

----oOo----

123

Under the old Cape Native Administration, Magistrates used to visit for long periods in their district. They travelled about and got to know the people under their administration. Such a magistrate was Mr W.P. Leary, who was Magistrate of the Mt Frere District, which was occupied by the Bhala tribe.

One day while he was in his garden, Tobela, appeared at his gate. After a friendly chat about the weather and crops, Tobela said: "I have known you, Leli, for a long time but you have never given me a present."

There was a hen scratching in the garden nearby, and Mr Leary said "You can have that hen if you can catch it" and then said jokingly "on the halves". Tobela caught the hen and went off very pleased.

Some years later Tobela again appeared at the gate. After greetings, he said to Mr Leary: "I have brought your cattle."

"My cattle! What do you mean" said Mr Leary.

"Well," said Tobela, "you gave me a hen on the halves and she had chickens. After a while I exchanged some fowls for a nanny goat. It bred well and I exchanged three goats for a heifer. It bred well and now I thought it was time I brought you your half share of the progeny and here they are – two tollies and a heifer."

Mr Leary was very taken aback, and was about to laugh the whole thing off. But that seemed very ungracious and hurtful, so he said "I'll take the red heifer and you can keep the two tollies." After commending Tobela for his faithfulness, Tobela and his son went off very happy at having the two tollies.

Mr Leary had a godson, Charlie H, a school friend of mine, to whom he gave the heifer, and when Charlie grew up and started farming, that heifer and her progeny formed the nucleus of his herd.

(Mr Leary's residence was on the outskirts of the village.)

----oOo----

When my father owned the farm Muratie at the foot of the Simonsberg, I lived at Rondebosch and sometimes went out to the farm for weekends.

I was leading a party climbing the Simonsberg and we were descending when a girl at the tail end of the party called for help. I could reach her only by climbing past the others. I took

hold of a rock to pull myself up, the rock came away and I fell on to a narrow hedge below. Fortunately, one of the party was just opposite and managed to grab my wrist. The rock must have passed over my legs as they were paralysed. With difficulty they got me down to where a horse could be brought.

I was quite all right the next day.

----oOo----

One of my farm labourers was a muscular Bhasa named Solurasha (the r was guttural). When there was team work he kept the others amused with his clowning. When we were burning firelines at night he used to sing, he had a deep organ like voice. Some of his songs caused great hilarity!

Except for an old overcoat in winter, he wore only a loin cloth. He was too thick set to be able to wear any of my cast-off clothing. He was overjoyed when a visitor gave him a wide pair of trousers. He waved them about and then proceeded to put them on back to front! He was a real heathen and took a delight in twitting the 'believers'.

He had had a month's leave, and as I rode past his huts on a Saturday, I stopped and said to him "Solurasha, your month's leave is up and I want you back to work on Monday".

He replied "Inkosi, I am building a hole for my fowls and need just one day to finish it. Let me have Monday and I'll come to work on Tuesday." I said "No, you are not a believer, you can finish your fowl hole on Sunday". "Yes, Inkosi," he said, "it is true that I am not a believer, but I believe that one should not work on Sunday"!

----o0o----

After Mr W.P. Leary retired from being Chief Magistrate of East Griqualand about 1950, he sometimes stayed with us at Inungi. He gave me some manuscripts of stories he had written. One of these was the story of Yalezo which follows. The date of the happenings described would have been about 1870.

Yalezo

I was a lad of about 14 years of age when I heard the story of Yalezo. Although it happened more than 60 years ago, I still remember every detail.

I was walking one hot summer's day in the Inku River near St Augustin's Mission Station, where I lived. Bathing near me were some native boys and I heard one of them say: "There goes Yalezo, let's get him to come and tell us the story of his adventures." I had heard of the exploits of this youth, and I welcomed the opportunity of hearing them from his own lips.

He was a lad of about 15 or 16 years of age, slight in build but muscular and wiry. Before embarking on his story it is necessary to give some idea of the background of the circumstances under which he lived.

Before 1865 the Pondo and Pondomisi tribes were living amicably alongside each other, the Ngcolara River being the boundary between them. In 1865 war broke out. Superior numbers enabled the Pondos to drive the smaller tribe across the Tzitza River, but the Pondomisi were stout fighters, and through the years of fights and raids that followed, they held their ground. The strip of country between the Ngcolara and Tzitza rivers remained unoccupied – a perilous no-man's land.

Raids to capture stock were carried out by both sides.

Women and girls were sometimes carried off and held to ransom. The captives were treated as guests and never interfered with. Negotiations for the ransoms were carried on by women from the kraals of the captives. The latter were sometimes given presents when they left.

These tribes, unlike the Zulus, never killed women and children in warfare.

Raids had to be carefully organised and were carried out by recognised leaders. When stock was captured, custom required that one or more head should be paid to the chief.

Yalezo, brought up in this atmosphere, was possessed with the desire to own a horse captured by himself, and he decided to make an incursion on his own.

Confiding in no-one, he set off alone and, keeping close cover crossed the Ngcolara River and entered the country of the warlike Pondos. Concealing himself in a koppie, he watched the kraals in the valley spread out below him. He noted several horses conveniently located for his purpose, and there being no-one in sight, he made his way towards them at dusk. Fortunately they stood still and he quickly succeeded in securing one.

He rode away through the night, crossed the Tzitza River early the next morning and reached home safely with his prize. But it was not to be his! To show disapproval, the horse was confiscated on behalf of the chief and Yalezo was left with nothing.

This did not deter him from setting out again. In drizzly and foggy weather, he entered the enemy country. He soon came up to a small troop of horses.

As he started to round these, up a man suddenly appeared ,who fortunately mistook him as being from his own kraal and told him to bring the horses in as night was falling. Yalezo turned the horses in the opposite direction. His course lay over the high ridge overlooking open country, towards where the present Tzitza bridge is situated. At that time it was thickly covered with mimosa trees, the grass was long and the night was dark and cold.

Daylight found him only as far as Umhlabati, the flat beyond which ran the Tzitza River. He had made repeated efforts to catch one or other of the horses but had failed.

He was now quite exhausted, famished and almost froze. At the Mbogotwana stream, he could get the horses no further. Leaving them he made his way to the nearest kraal across the Tzitza.

The occupants of the kraal went to where he had left the horses, but they had turned back and made for home, being met by the owners who had followed the spoor.

The Chief Umhlohlo – later notorious for the murder of the Magistrate Hope and his companions – sent a warning to Yalezo's father to the effect that was a man's game, not a boy's, and he must put a stop to his son's foolhardy expeditions.

Yalezo lay low for a while, but he could not resist the urging of a young man named Kayisa that they should set out together on a horse raiding expedition. On reaching the enemy country, they hid in a patch of bush. Now natives living on the borders of the territory occupied by this tribe made it a practice to beat the forests in the vicinity of their kraals, not only for hunting game ,but also to ensure that no enemy spies or stock lifters were lurking in the neighbourhood. There was such a hunt this day and the patch of bush in which they were hiding was the first to be hunted. The dogs soon drew attention to their presence. They were surrounded and captured and taken before the local headman by whom a report was sent to the Chief.

Pending the reply from the Chief, Yalezo was not deterred by the seriousness of his position from enjoying the hospitality of his captors and he shared in the feast of meat and beer. Poor Kayisa was assumed to be the notorious Yalezo and was buffeted by the women and taunted with having brought a child into such trouble.

The messenger to the Chief returned with orders that they must be executed, and the following morning they were taken by a body of men to a spot where the Ngcolosa, after going over a waterfall, runs between high krantzes (*crags*).

Local Chief Oakaza deputed two men to carry out the execution. Each had to take his victim to the edge of the krantz, hit him on the head with a bunguza *(a heavy knobkerrie)* and throw him over the krantz. This procedure was carried out with Kayisa.

Yalezo, as soon as his executioner raised his bunguza, sprang at him and dragged him towards the edge of the krantz. The man struggled away and Yalezo, turning again to the edge, saw a scrubby tree growing out of a ledge some way down. Without hesitating, he jumped and managed to land in the tree. Grabbing the branches, he broke his fall. He made a perilous descent the rest of the way down, scratched and bruised, but uninjured. He quickly made off downstream in full view of his would-be executioners, who hurried off in a circuitous route to reach the valley below. As soon as Yalezo saw them disappear from the top of the krantz, he doubled back in the scrub while his enemies rushed off in the direction they had seen him running. Making use of cover, he reached a stony koppie whence he could see the search for himself being conducted in the distance.

When night fell, he went on to a trader's store. After resting there for a day, he went to the Shawbury Mission and thence home. The affair was reported to the chief, and Yalezo's father was fined and told that there would be trouble for him if Yalezo's ventures did not cease. One wonders what the future held for Yalezo!

Descendant trees
Sir Walter and Lady Stanford's Children

DESCENDANTS OF WALTER ELLIOT STANFORD

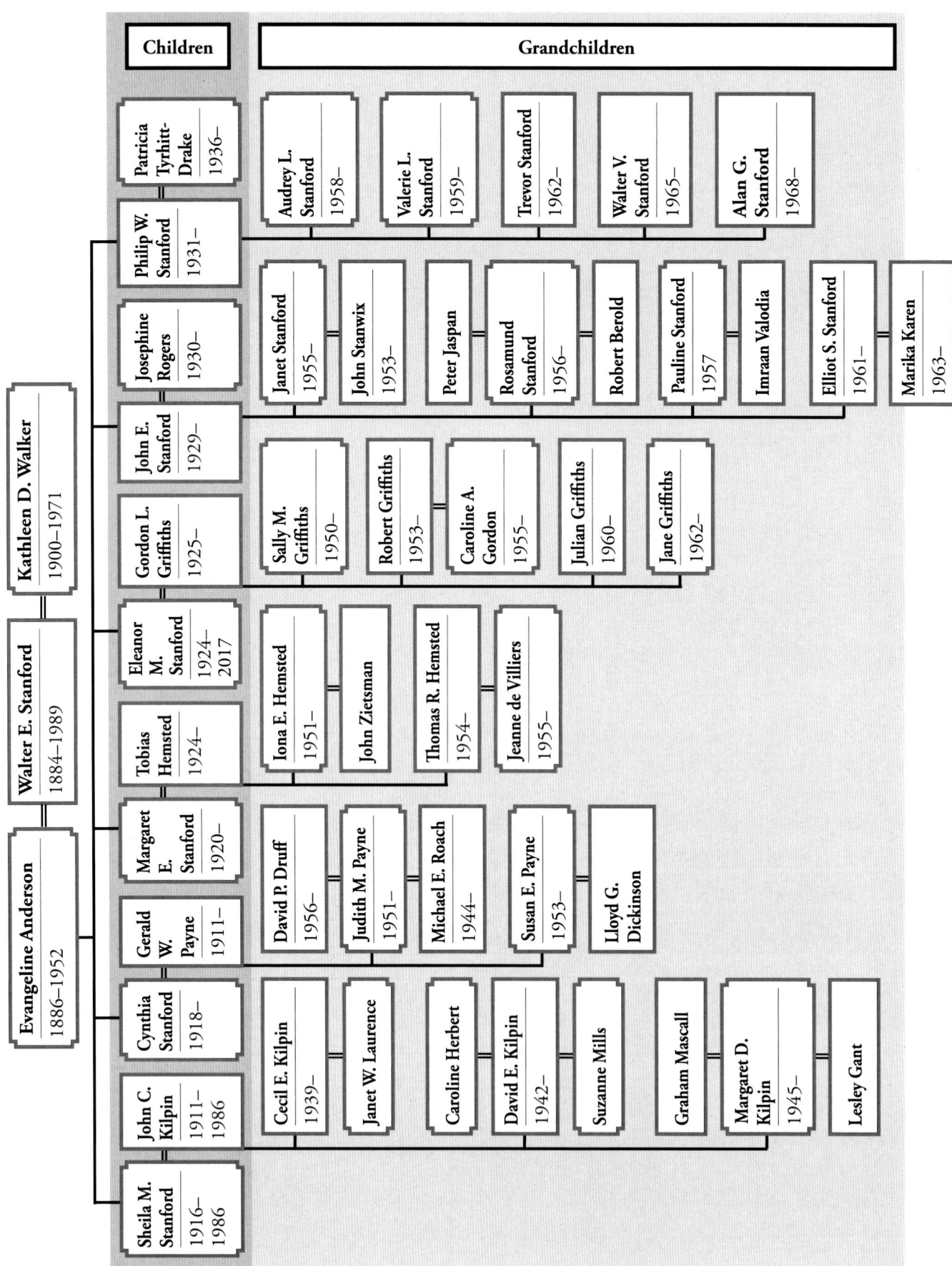

DESCENDANTS OF DOROTHY MAUD STANFORD

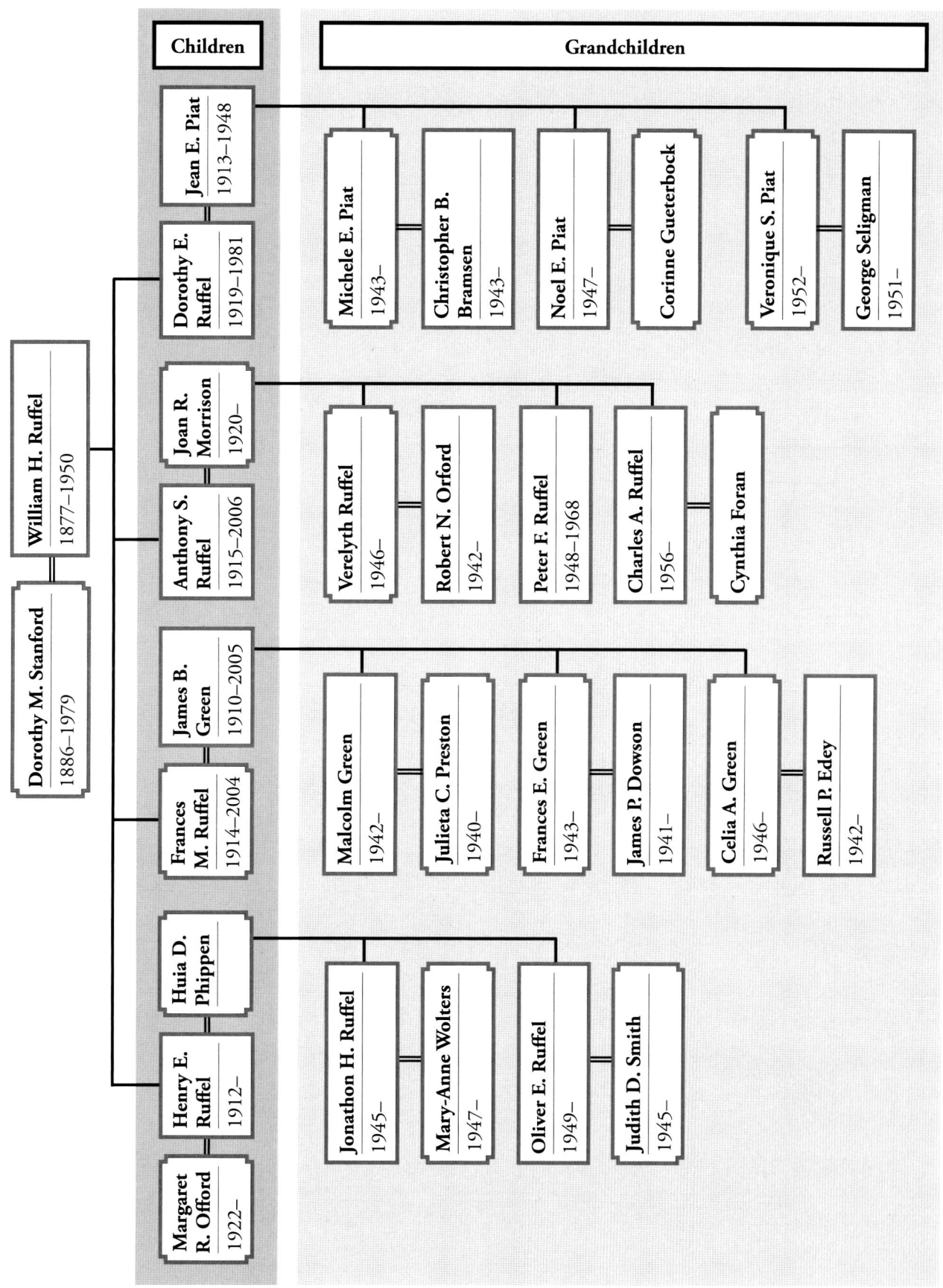

DESCENDANTS OF ALICE MINNIE STANFORD

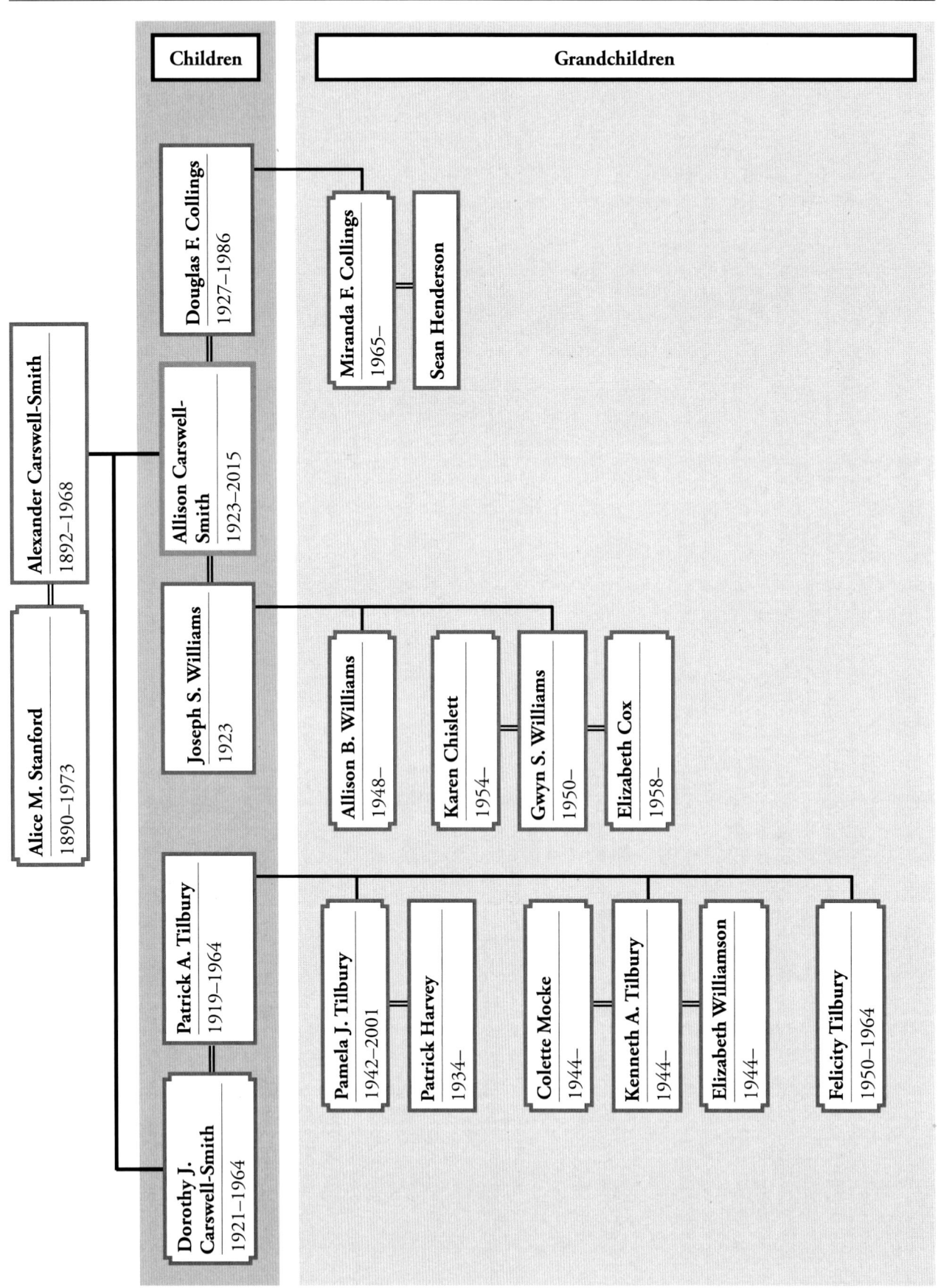

Children

Grandchildren

Alexander Carswell-Smith
1892–1968

Alice M. Stanford
1890–1973

Douglas F. Collings
1927–1986

Miranda F. Collings
1965–

Sean Henderson

Allison Carswell-Smith
1923–2015

Joseph S. Williams
1923

Allison B. Williams
1948–

Karen Chislett
1954–

Gwyn S. Williams
1950–

Elizabeth Cox
1958–

Patrick A. Tilbury
1919–1964

Dorothy J. Carswell-Smith
1921–1964

Pamela J. Tilbury
1942–2001

Patrick Harvey
1934–

Colette Mocke
1944–

Kenneth A. Tilbury
1944–

Elizabeth Williamson
1944–

Felicity Tilbury
1950–1964

DESCENDANTS OF ARTHUR WARNER STANFORD

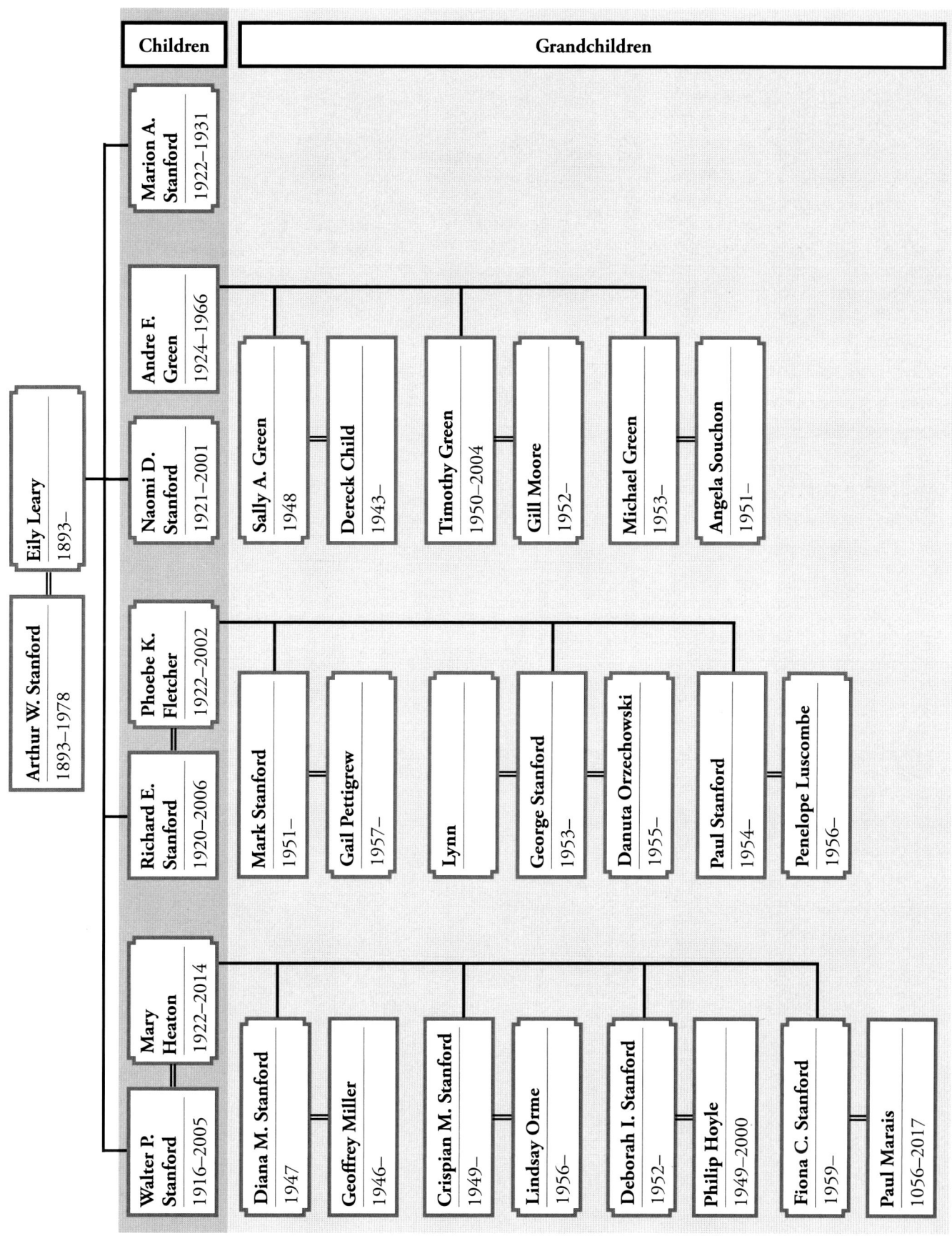

Children	Grandchildren

Eily Leary
1893–

Arthur W. Stanford
1893–1978

Marion A. Stanford
1922–1931

Andre F. Green
1924–1966

Naomi D. Stanford
1921–2001

Sally A. Green
1948

Dereck Child
1943–

Timothy Green
1950–2004

Gill Moore
1952–

Michael Green
1953–

Angela Souchon
1951–

Phoebe K. Fletcher
1922–2002

Richard E. Stanford
1920–2006

Mark Stanford
1951–

Gail Pettigrew
1957–

Lynn

George Stanford
1953–

Danuta Orzechowski
1955–

Paul Stanford
1954–

Penelope Luscombe
1956–

Mary Heaton
1922–2014

Walter P. Stanford
1916–2005

Diana M. Stanford
1947

Geoffrey Miller
1946–

Crispian M. Stanford
1949–

Lindsay Orme
1956–

Deborah I. Stanford
1952–

Philip Hoyle
1949–2000

Fiona C. Stanford
1959–

Paul Marais
1056–2017

DESCENDANTS OF HELEN ROSE STANFORD

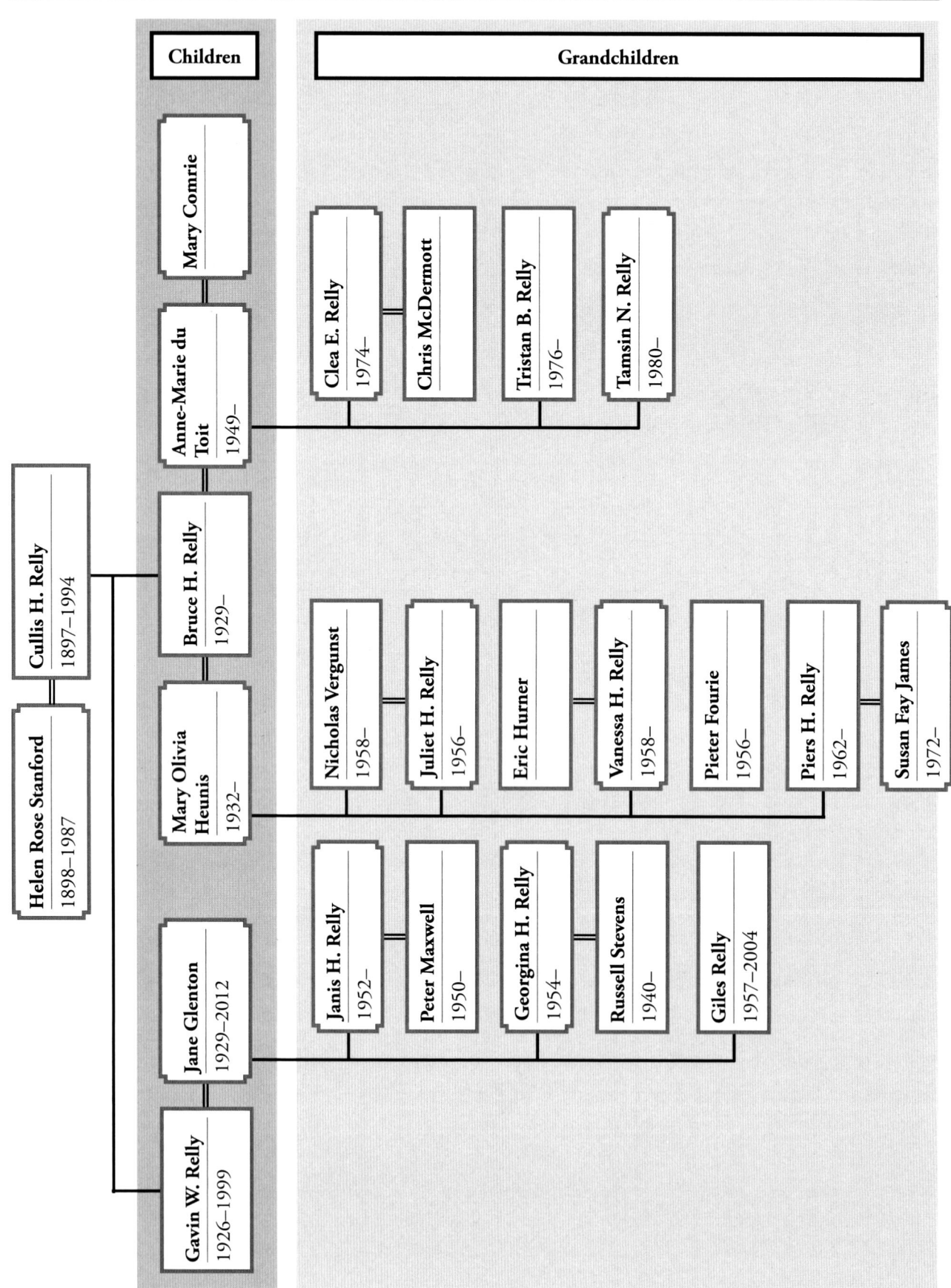

DESCENDANTS OF EILEEN MARY STANFORD

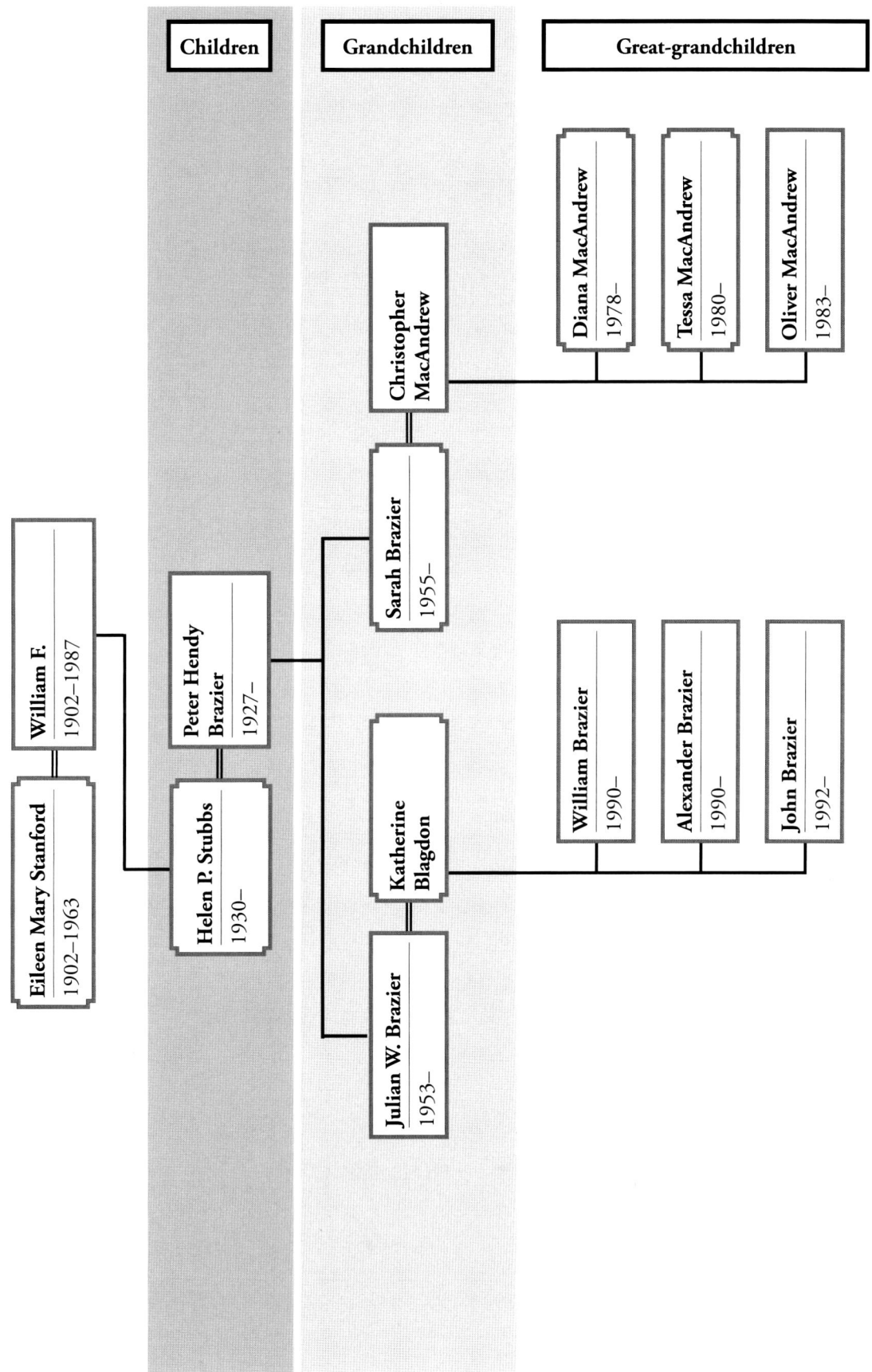

Children	Grandchildren	Great-grandchildren

William F.
1902–1987

Eileen Mary Stanford
1902–1963

Peter Hendy Brazier
1927–

Helen P. Stubbs
1930–

Sarah Brazier
1955–

Christopher MacAndrew

Julian W. Brazier
1953–

Katherine Blagdon

Diana MacAndrew
1978–

Tessa MacAndrew
1980–

Oliver MacAndrew
1983–

William Brazier
1990–

Alexander Brazier
1990–

John Brazier
1992–

Bibliography

I have drawn facts and materials from the following sources:

University of Cape Town Archives – The Stanford Papers (BC293).

The Reminiscences of Sir Walter Stanford Vol. 1 1850-1885; edited by J.W. Macquarrie, The Van Riebeeck Society, Cape Town, 1958.

The Reminiscences of Sir Walter Stanford Vol. 2 1885-1929; edited by J.W. Macquarrie, The Van Riebeeck Society, Cape Town, 1962.

The Inner History of the National Convention; Sir Edgar Walton, Maskew Miller, Cape Town, 1912.

Thomas Holden Bowker – His reminiscences, Last Days in England; www.eggsa.org/1820Settlers '1820 .

Settler correspondence as preserved in National Archives; Kew; edited by Sue Mackay.

The Settler Handbook; M.D. Nash, Chameleon Press, Cape Town, 1987.

Pawns in a Larger Game – Life on the Eastern Cape Frontier; A.D.M. Walker, (Calamaish Books, Durban 2013.

They Came from a Far Land; May Bell, Maskew Miller, Cape Town, 1963.

An Introduction to South African Methodists, Prof Leslie Hewson, Standard Press, Cape Town ,1950.

Clarence Jenkins Warner – from a report lodged in the Albany Museum, Grahamstown, in 1970 by D.H. Patrick R.M.L. Also submitted by P.J. Potgieter to the March 1961 issue of the *baNtu*.

A Beautiful Country – People and Places of East Griqualand; Milner Snell, Kokstad, 2012.

Thus Came the English 1820; Dorothy E. Rivett-Carnac, Howard Timmins, Cape Town 1963.

Sir Walter Stanford – A voice of the future in the National Convention; Randolph Vigne, Quarterly Bulletin of the National Library of South Africa; Jul-Sep 2010, Vol. 64 Issue 3, p117.

Contemporaneous newspaper reports and obituaries.

The extensive family trees were drawn by my Grandmother, Dorothy Maud Ruffel (née Stanford).

Family archives of photographs, letters and writings.

Memories and family anecdotes contributed by many of the wider family, including:
Michele Bo Bramsen; Helen Pat Brazier; Allison Carswell-Smith; Frances Dowson; Micky Gant; Lois Green; Malcolm Green; Sheila Kilpin; Diana Miller; Bruce Relly; John Stanford; Cynthia Payne; Bronwyn Williams; Georgina Relly; Jan Relly; Veronique Seligman; Debbie Hoyle; Jonathon Ruffel; Oliver Ruffel and many others.

Illustrations and Photographs

Most of the photographs come from family albums or collections, and have been scanned or photographed by the author.

Of the remaining illustrations and photographs, the author has used three sources:
- *The Reminiscences of Sir Walter Stanford Vol. 1 & 11 1850-1885*; edited by J.W. Macquarrie, The Van Riebeeck Society, Cape Town, 1958
- Sir WEM Stanford Papers, manuscripts and archives, University of Cape Town Libraries, BC 293
- Online resources in the public domain. Individual sources are listed below.

Thomas Baines painting (back cover)
Thomas Baines – Suid-Afrikaanse Geskiedenis in Beeld; Anthony Preston. Bion Books, South Africa, 1989. Believed to be on display at the Albany Museum, Grahamstown. Public Domain, https://commons. wikimedia.org/w/index.php?curid=3737884

Lord Charles Somerset (p11)
https://commons.wikimedia.org/w/index.php?curid=52930198

The *Weymouth* (p12)
http://www.southafricansettlers.com/wp-content/themes/pretty-parchment/images/weymouth_ship.png

Settlers arriving in Algoa Bay, 1820 (p13)
https://samsterwasi.files.wordpress.com/2014/11/1820settlers.jpg

Map of Albany Settlement (p14)
https://s-media-cache-ak0.pinimg.com/originals/a6/b9/d9/a6b9d9b6acded51115957212656822c4.jpg

George Wood (p26)
http://1820settlers.com/genealogy/Media/pictures/Wood_George_Alfred_%5B931%5D.jpg

Lovedale Missionary Institution (p41)
By The National Archives UK, OGL, https://commons.wikimedia.org/w/index.php?curid=19280954

Sigcau, Chief of the Pondos (p51)
Illustration for *The Graphic*, 13 April 1895, © Look and Learn.

Sir Henry de Villiers (p51)
https://upload.wikimedia.org/wikipedia/af/3/34/Sir_Henry_de_Villiers.jpg

William Philip Schreiner (p54)
Elliott & Fry [Public domain], Afrikana Museum, Johannesburg, via Wikimedia Commons https://upload. wikimedia.org/wikipedia/commons/8/8d/William_Philip_Schreiner00.jpg

Sir Walter and Lady Stanford, Golden Wedding (p61)
Sir Walter and Lady Stanford, June 1933. Copy of *Cape Times* photo. BC 293 – G32 Sir WEM Stanford
Papers, Manuscripts & Archives, University of Cape Town Libraries

Portrait of Celia Edey (p99)
From the studio of Nicola Green

E.J. Warner gravestone (p103)
https://en.wikipedia.org/wiki/South_Africa_Act_1909

Emma Ruth Warner (p103)
http://genealogy.amay.co.uk/images/WF5-EmmaRuthWarner.jpg